Contents

Contents

General Editor's Preface

Schooling is one of the activities of a *good* society. It is one way among others of providing for the welfare of the people. But the processes and preoccupations of schooling have not always ensured that the welfare of those in school is catered for in any direct and positive way. It is about the positive ways which schools may employ that this book is concerned.

The eleven original contributions to this book range across the many issues of schooling and welfare and do so with great insight and humanity, and from many points of view; including those of head-teacher, pupils and staff. But the main value of the contributions to this book is the questions which they raise about the responsibilities of the schools and those who work in them for the well-being of those conscripted beneficiaries, the pupils, who spend so much of their formative years in them. The modern world can be neglectful of welfare, making it a personal not a social responsibility. It is such a view from the schools that this book most emphatically, and rightly, rejects.

In every respect this book is not only a welcome addition to the literature, it is also a substantive contribution to our understanding of the intimate and necessary relationship of schooling and welfare.

P.H. Taylor
University of Birmingham 1985

Editorial: Three Reasons for Thinking More About Schooling and Welfare

The idea that schools ought to be engaged in more than just the intellectual and cognitive development of pupils has long been recognized in many countries (Lang and Ribbins, 1985). In Britain during the late 1940s the term 'pastoral care' began to be used in schools by teachers to categorize the multifarious welfare activities they undertook on behalf of pupils. A number of efforts have been made to clarify our understanding of 'pastoral care' in education and at least one tentative 'map of the field' has been attempted (Ribbins and Best, 1985). Despite its evident significance, rather less attention has been devoted to explorations of the meanings which might be attached to 'welfare' as applied to educational contexts. Thus it remains an influential, much used, yet essentially shadowy concept employed to account for and justify a variety of more or less compatible purposes and practices within the contemporary school.

In inviting a number of people to think about aspects of the relationship between schooling and welfare I deliberately resisted, sometimes with some difficulty, the temptation to offer an editorial line on how the term was to be interpreted and defined. What I did ask, however, was that they all gave this issue some attention in the hope that such an approach might identify and illustrate some key differences in usage and thus, hopefully, to initiate further debate on the issues involved. Such a debate seems necessary for a number of reasons, of which I shall discuss just *three*.

First, because we need to think about the consequences for education and for schooling of the kinds of changes which may be taking place in the economy and society. Watts (1983) considers one such issue in his study of *Education, Unemployment and the Future of Work*. In this he examines various senarios ('employment' or 'unemployment', 'leisure' or 'work') and their implications for education and for schools and teachers. As he remarks, it may well be that the most important question we should be asking, 'is how education can help people to construct a satisfying lifestyle and social identity without work' (p. 179). This kind of question raises as many problems about welfare as it does about education and may even suggest that to have a concern for welfare is to have a concern for the purposes and practices of education as a whole rather than with an identifiable and distinct aspect of schooling in particular.

Secondly, we may also have to think about what tasks schools ought to be engaged in. Pring (1984) makes the point that:

> Teachers are having to take on responsibilities that are often more concerned with social welfare than with education. Why is that? First, schools are frequently the only places where children who are suffering from a wide range of social and medical disadvantages can find someone who is caring and intelligent to talk to and to get help from ... Secondly, a precondition of successful teaching is that the learners have the preconditions of successful learning ... Thirdly, the world that young people are entering into is an increasingly complex one in which they will need guidance (p. 141, 142).

What is clear is that not all teachers view such developments with equanimity as a number of studies have shown. Thus, at 'Deanswater' one member of the staff remarked sourly that 'All teachers have become tutors' and 'tutors have become father confessor, confidant, disciplinarian, policeman, probation officer, amateur psychologist, sports enthusiast — everything!' (Ribbins and Ribbins, 1984). Mclaughlin (1983) in an examination of the welfare dimension of schooling as expressed in such ideas as 'pastoral care' and 'the pastoral curriculum' warns that 'In my view the pastoral curriculum cannot be seen as the *prime* responsibility of the school. The central educational task is to provide a broad, general education' (p. 98). He proposes a set of principles which might be invoked by a school to determine the scope and content of its efforts relevant to the aim of meeting 'the personal needs of pupils' resolving their individual problems, making informed decisions and taking their place in their personal and social world' (Marland, 1980 p. 157):

1 That the pupil be equipped to deal with a range of problems, decisions and adjustments that are likely to confront any person in our society;
2 That the ability of pupils to deal with such problems,

decisions etc. are not likely to be brought about by other means;

3 That the school and its teachers have the expertise to offer;
4 That dealing with such a programme does not get in the way of the school's central task — the provision of a liberal education (Mclaughlin, 1983, p. 95).

Thirdly, because although a debate on the notion of 'welfare' in an educational context may not establish a consensus on the conceptual, normative and empirical issues involved it may serve to establish some measure of agreement, however crude, as to the main alternative usages. To an extent it is possible to identify some distinctions which are already to be found in the literature.

One example of such distinctions is a continuum of usage with at one polar extreme the view that the welfare task of the school is *primary*. This view is epitomized in what we have described elsewhere as the 'conventional wisdom' of 'pastoral care' (Best *et al*, 1977). Marland (1974), for example, has argued that the school would not be an effective vehicle for handing on the complex culture of society 'if it does not help the individual pupil to find himself, and find meaning for his studies and his life. To do this, the *central task of the school, its pastoral work*, must be sensitive, warm, human, efficient, realistic and thorough' (p. 11–12, my italics). At the other polar extreme are ideas which deny that welfare is a necessary or even a proper task for schools or teachers to engage in. A view trenchantly expressed by a teacher at 'Deanswater', 'a teacher should be a teacher. An adult with a mastery of his subject and a trained skill in imparting it. That surely is a sufficient contribution to society — more is self deluding folly' (Ribbins and Ribbins, 1984, p. 17). Other teachers at the school adopted a less extreme view arguing that, although the welfare dimension of schooling was important, yet 'Pastoral care must be related primarily to the academic needs of the school' or that 'Pastoral care should principally be about supporting learning . . . Pastoral care should give a lot of support to the academic needs of the school' (ibid). Such a view is also taken by some of the most influential theorists of 'pastoral care'. Hamblin (1978), for example, stresses the need 'for a carefully planned integration of the pastoral and curricular aspects of the comprehensive school based on the realization that the true failure of the secondary school lies in the field of learning' (p. 1) and his emphasis is on the role which pastoral care can play as a facilitator of the schools effective academic work. Mclaughlin (1983), as we saw earlier, also rejects the notion that the pastoral or welfare tasks of the school are its prime responsibility.

Another set of distinctions turns upon the extent to which the welfare aspect of schooling is seen as something to do with the school as a whole or as a particular aspect or dimension of it. The former view is likely to be adopted by those who see the pastoral task of the school as central and they usually express this view by rejecting what they categorize as the 'pastoral-academic' split (see Best and Ribbins, 1983). We have ourselves taken the view that it is useful to distinguish the pastoral dimension of schooling (with its welfare functions) from the academic and disciplinary (Best *et al*, 1983). In one of the papers in this volume, Neville Jones seems to take yet another view and regards 'welfare' as an added or extra dimension of provision made by the pastoral systems of schools for those children who have a special need for it.

The following papers address themselves to these and other issues. In the first of the papers Ron Best and Steve Decker attempt a fundamental re-examination of the pastoral and welfare purposes of schooling and argue that even the most radical and critical of writings now available whilst they try to bring rhetoric and reality a bit closer, do not challenge the basic structures and functions of schooling, assume a gradualist stance and stop well short of a full-blooded Marxist or Progressivist analysis. This criticism is well justified and the examination attempted by Best and Decker is long overdue. In the final paper, Hywel Thomas, an economist with a special interest in educational administration and policy making, adopts a definition of 'welfare' which takes the concept back to its economic roots and which is quite different and significantly wider than that taken by other contributors to this book. In his analysis he stresses the need for greater prominence to be given to an individual welfare principle expressed in a greater degree of choice for children and suggests what the implications of such a principle would be for the curriculum and organization of schooling.

Three further papers consider the relationship of the welfare dimension of schooling to other aspects of schooling and to the wider welfare network. Ribbins outlines a model of schooling designed to relate the pastoral, academic and disciplinary dimensions of schooling to the good of the pupil conceived in terms of the contribution which they make to the welfare and education of the individual child and to the maintenance of that irreducible minimum of order without which any kind of social life would be impossible. This model is then used to relate the various ideas and concepts about 'personal, social and moral education', 'the pastoral curriculum' and 'tutorial programmes' to each other and to the more fundamental dimensions of schooling. A case is made out for the implementation of a 'welfare curriculum' in schools. Tattum's paper deals with the vexed issues of care and control in education, a topic at the heart of much practitioner concern. He offers a number of suggestions as to what a constructive approach to discipline might look like. John Welton considers the extent to which effective welfare provision within schools and in the wider welfare network is inhibited by interprofessional mistrust and misunderstanding. He warns that teachers must not stand apart from other caring professions if things are to improve.

A third set of papers focuses upon the three main groups most closely concerned with welfare in schools — pupils, parents and teachers. Peter Lang argues that those involved in the provision of welfare in schools sometimes have oversimplified and stereotyped views about pupils' needs and understandings and that this may be explained by to the fact that little attention has been given to what pupils think and want. Parents constitute another group whose concern for the welfare dimension of schooling is commonly under-valued by teachers. In his paper Marland identifies and challenges two historical myths that teachers all too often hold — that schools are omnipotent and that parents are inadequate. He suggests twenty specific acts, activities and policies which schools will need to imple-ment if teachers are to involve parents in a genuine partnership in providing for the welfare needs of pupils. Finally, Robert Laslett extends an influential analysis initially proposed by Williamson by considering the welfare needs of teachers as a way of facilitating the pastoral needs of children.

The last group of papers consider the educational and welfare needs of groups of children categorized as 'remedial' or as 'special needs'. For the last few years Ron Best has been researching into the grounds upon which some children are designated as 'remedial' and what the consequences are for them of such a designation. He challenges the essentially psychological premises upon which con-ventional thinking about remedial education are based and explores some of the confusions that abound in the language of discourse in this area. Neville Jones shares some of the same concerns in his analysis of thinking about the child categorized as having special needs. As Oxfordshire's senior educational psychologist he has been closely involved with the integration issue in the Post-Warnock era and has some criticisms to make of the 1981 Act. This, he feels, tends to sustain an unhelpful dichotomy between those children seen as having a 'special need' and those who are 'normal', in the terms of the new vocabulary between those who are 'statemented' and those who are not. Again, like Ron Best he questions the value of such categorizations and presses instead for a commitment to the worth of each child's development within the context of an integrated system of provision as far as this is reasonably possible. Finally, Keith Blackburn, drawing on the wealth of his experience and thinking, asks us to think hard about what experiences we provide for children and about what they learn from the contemporary school. As do many of the authors in this book, he points to a tendency which schools have to locate pupil problems within the pupils themselves (or their families) and a reluctance to ask to what extent it is that schools and teachers contribute significantly to such problems.

At the outset I had hoped that a very tentative 'map of the field' might emerge from this venture. It could be that one might be extracted from the papers in this volume and elsewhere. But, as yet, such an endeavour seems premature and may obscure as much as it reveals. If *Schooling and Welfare* has challenged some received wisdoms, identified some interesting questions and possible answers, and stimulates further research and thinking about the issues involved, this will be justification enough.

Pastoral Care and Welfare: Some Underlying Issues

Ron Best and Steve Decker
Chelmer Institute of Higher Education

Introduction

Recent research in education has demonstrated the diversity of perspectives from which teachers (Best *et al.* 1983) and pupils (Lang, 1983) view 'pastoral care', and there is a growing interest amongst philosophers of education in unravelling the concept itself and what its implications for the school curriculum might be (Dooley 1980, McLaughlin 1982, Elliot 1982, Hibberd 1983). This interest is somewhat overdue, but welcome nonetheless, for pastoral care has long been a major aspect of institutionalized schooling (Lang 1984), even if it is only in the last two decades that it has assumed structural significance in the form of vertical, horizontal and matrix systems in comprehensive schools. While some have found considerable appeal in the existence of a variety of perspectives on helping children (Johnson *et al.* 1980), it seems to others (Best *et al.* 1983, Murgatroyd 1980) that there are dangers in embracing too easily a pluralism which reflects a lack of consensus about what is the proper concern of teachers, and therefore raises doubts about the possibility of a concerted and effective welfare effort on the part of schools. However, a greater danger seems to lie in the complacency of those headteachers and other educational decision-makers who simply assume that their views are shared by everyone else. To base educational planning upon such an assumption is naive.

Our intention in this paper is to clarify and make explicit some of the things which are implicit in the variety of views which are held about pastoral care and of its relation to the academic work of the school. We shall suggest that these views and the assumptions and values which underpin them, do not exist in a vacuum, but are located in a particular social, historical and political context and find expression as part of a stream of consciousness or evolution of ideas of a particular culture. In particular, we shall argue that the thought and action which is normally identified with 'pastoral care' in schools may be seen as a specific educational instance of a more general climate of values and ideas. It is the development of those ideas and values which is embodied in, underpins, and to some extent accounts for, the development of the prevailing social arrangements which we know as 'the welfare state'.

In saying this, we are intentionally drawing attention to the fact that there are moral and political values of the most fundamental sort at the root of any institutionalized system of caring. And if informed discussion and rational planning of pastoral care in schools is to be possible, those involved must recognize that this is so. Because social policy at all levels entails profound but challenging values, the formulation of pastoral care policies can never be a simple matter: at rock-bottom it entails a consideration of the deepest issues about the nature of Man and Society.

Section 1:   Perspectives on Welfare

Perspectives on pastoral care, therefore, are perspectives on the desirability and possibility of development of human welfare. We can explore attitudes to the role of schools as agents of care by looking at the variety of perspectives which have been (and are) adopted towards the development and efficacy of the welfare state.

In their book *Ideology and Social Welfare*, George and Wilding (1976) examine these perspectives by looking at the positions of a range of thinkers from Milton Friedman (on the Right) to Ralph Miliband (on the Left). Despite the variations between individuals, they argue that more than enough common ground can be identified to permit their classification into four broad groups: the Anti-Collectivists, the Reluctant Collectivists, the Fabian Socialists, and the Marxists. Their positions, as described by George and Wilding, can be briefly summarized as follows:

(a)   The Anti-Collectivists

For the Anti-Collectivists, 'Freedom or liberty, individualism and inequality are the fundamental social values ...' (p. 22). 'Liberty', in this context, is conceived in negative terms as 'the absence of coercion' (*ibid*), and is seen as leading to the individual 'exerting himself to the utmost of his abilities to the advantage of himself and his country. Individualism is complementary to freedom and one cannot exist without the other' (p. 23). Collective controls are therefore perceived as an unacceptable constraint and vigorously rejected as 'government coercion' (p. 25).

Since Liberty thus conceived includes the freedom to strive for treasured goals and to dispose of one's wealth as one pleases, the inequality inherent in the existence of social classes and the related occupation structure is both accepted and defended. Since incentives would suffer, and because of the disruption resulting from 'the abolition of social esteem attached to different occupations which acts as a guide for recruiting people to those occupations . . .', Equality is as economically unacceptable as it is politically. Thus ideological as well as pragmatic justifications are employed in the rejection of collectivism generally, based, the authors suggest, on a 'four-fold assertion . . . : It is feared that substantial government intervention is socially disruptive, it is wasteful of resources, it promotes inefficiency and it obliterates individual freedom' (p. 27).

The Anti-Collectivists' objections to the welfare state are a natural enough consequence of such thinking and it is clear that their objections are deeply rooted in their economic and political ideology. It is not only that their rejection of welfare measures reflects the above values; it also reflects deeper fears about the relationship between social engineering and ultimate political destinations:

> The Welfare State . . . has been fraudulently created by well-meaning, but misguided, reformers capitalizing on the rising aspirations of an unthinking general public. The Welfare State is, in embryo, a socialist state . . . (p. 33).

(b)   The Reluctant Collectivists

While sharing the Anti-Collectivists' basic beliefs in liberty, individualism and competitive private enterprise, this group is willing to countenance collective intervention on pragmatic and humanitarian grounds. While continuing 'to believe that capitalism is the best economic system, . . . they believe that to function efficiently and fairly it requires judicious regulation and control. Its faults are serious, but not fundamental; they can be corrected' (p. 42). While the Anti-Collectivists offer a four-fold criticism of state-intervention, this group offer four criticisms of capitalism, which, whatever the scale of their essential conservatism, they perceive as necessitating precisely such intervention. These criticisms are 'that capitalism is not self-regulating; it is wasteful and inefficient and misallocates resources; it will not of itself abolish injustice and poverty; (and) it leads to dominant economic interests being identified as the national interest' (p. 45).

The State must intervene on humanitarian grounds, since human welfare must not be allowed to suffer because of imperfections in a basically appropriate 'machine'. Moreover, since questions of social priority are involved, and since only the state can make decisions about such priorities and formulate 'guidelines' for welfare provision, government involvement simply cannot be avoided. But as it is only the *imperfections* in the free-enterprise system for which compensation is needed, collectivization of the efficient aspects of private enterprise is not acceptable. Thus, in Beveridge's plan for social insurance, the aim was to abolish want by establishing a necessary minimum, *above which* distribution of wealth was for the market to determine. As George and Wilding summarize:

> The aim of the reluctant collectivists is to purge capitalism of its inefficiencies and its injustices so that it may survive. They believe that capitalism and planning are compatible, that government intervention is necessary to make capitalism morally acceptable. Their achievement has been to save capitalism and to preserve its essential elements while reducing or eliminating what has become unacceptable (p. 61).

(c)   *The Fabian Socialists*

While boundaries are not always clear, this group distinguishes itself from the Reluctant Collectivists by their emphasis upon *equality*, and by their fundamental rejection of capitalism in favour of socialism. Their attitude to state intervention is most assuredly positive.

If the Anti-Collectivists stress liberty, inequality and individualism, the central values of this group are 'equality, freedom and fellowship' (p. 62). However, even for the Fabian Socialists, equality is not unqualified. Though denying that it is sufficient in itself, it is 'equality of opportunity' that has most often triumphed over equality of wealth or income, and in this way the existing social scale of occupation/income/quality-of-life has been at least tacitly endorsed. What is sought are equalizing measures which will reduce somewhat the extremes of inequality, and upon this narrowed scale to create a meritocracy such that one's position on it at least reflects ability and effort, and in the process avoid the grosser wastages of human talent.

'Fellowship' or 'fraternity' are equatable with a commitment to *co-operation* as against competition, and it is this and not 'charity' that is seen as the logical consequence of humanitarian sentiments. Indeed, 'charity' is not even a natural accompaniment to the free-market system which, after all, enshrines self-interest as the guiding value of society. Moreover, the system is 'undemocratic', 'unjust', 'inefficient', and 'has not, will not, and cannot abolish poverty let alone inequality' (pp. 70–1).

The tasks of government are therefore clear: to weigh up competing social costs and benefits of alternative economic policies, and then 'to ensure that industry operates in the light of social need rather than self interest' (p. 73). The state must concern itself with modifying the distribution of wealth and life-changes, but also with the distribution of power and freedom: the latter must also be planned for and not sacrificed to centralist tyranny. 'The socialist's attitude towards the welfare state is one of enthusiastic approval and support' (p. 74). It is part of a 'gradualism' — 'pragmatic, piecemeal social engineering' (p. 75) — which has become a central feature of British society, and whose existence is to some extent accepted, however reluctantly, across the broad 'middle-ground' of the political spectrum. It is not, however, without its limitations, voiced by the Fabians as four general fears: 'that it is concerned with injustice rather than justice, that it can be used by government as a substitute for the necessary preventive action, that it can be limited to seeking equality of opportunity, that it is concerned with poverty not with inequality' (p. 80). These criticisms figure prominently in the ideology of the fourth of George and Wilding's groups: the Marxists.

(d)   The Marxists

As Arblaster (cited p. 88) has argued, what distinguishes separate political positions is not necessarily that they espouse different values: rather it is the fact that they differ markedly in their interpretations of those values and the priority they give to them. This can be clearly seen in the present context, where the Marxists, too, hold 'equality' and 'fraternity' to be important, but in common with their avowed enemies, the Anti-Collectivists, also claim allegiance to 'liberty'.

However, they do not accept , with the Fabians, that 'equality' can be rendered as 'equality of opportunity', nor, with the Anti-Collectivists, the negative concept of 'freedom *from* ...' which they supplant with a positive notion of 'freedom *to* ...'. That is to say, man's essential humanity is realizable through, not the absence of coercion, but the existence of conditions — and these may well include restraints — within which a life of physical, mental (and, perhaps, spiritual) fulfilment is possible.

Both liberty and equality, moreover, must be seen together with 'fraternity' as essential to one another's existence. There can be no real freedom without a reduction in the grosser inequalities — and that means a fundamental change in economic arrangements — while 'fraternity' here conveys a conviction that, if granted a freedom purged of privilege and the right to exploit others, people will, as a matter of fact, live 'harmoniously and co-operatively with each other' (Arblaster, quoted p. 88). Thus, the Marxist conception of Liberty is antithetical to the individualism of the anti-collectivists.

For the Marxists, the fundamental dimension of social life — and the 'prime mover' of change — is the economy. Whatever caveats of 'relative autonomy' may be introduced, it is the economic structure of production, distribution and exchange from which the social and political structures take their shape, and which determines the content of the ideas, attitudes and beliefs of the cultural superstructure within which these structures find legitimation.

From the last point it follows that 'the State apparatus is not a neutral umpire, arbitrating impartially between competing groups' (p. 91). Rather, it represents the interests of the ruling class: only in 'an egalitarian, undifferentiated society' could it be otherwise (*ibid*). And since it is private ownership of the means of production from which the features of an *in*egalitarian and stratified society spring, the communization of the means of production is an essential pre-requisite for a just and impartial government. In alleviating the extremes of inequality, poverty and squalour, *within* a basically capitalist system, the welfare state is seen by some Marxists as the product of concessions made by the ruling class in order to blunt the blade of revolution. Other Marxists do not agree, however, preferring to see welfare provisions as a series of hard-won gains resulting from actual and potential working-class pressure within what is ultimately a struggle between broad social and economic groups.

Unlike the Fabians, the Marxists 'maintain that the welfare state, by its very nature, cannot abolish poverty and inequality . . . because to do so would imply a defeat of the ruling class. It may modify but it cannot solve the main social problems for these are rooted in the class structure of society' (p. 104). In short, expediency and compromise in the Fabian policies of the mixed economy and the limited collectivization of welfare provision 'have delayed and perhaps made impossible the creation of a socialist state in this country' (p. 85).

Section 2: Models of Man

Underlying each of these positions on the desirability or otherwise of organized welfare provision are distinctive models of man and of the nature of human action. These models may not be explicitly formulated in the thoughts and proclamations of the protagonists, but are no less significant as assumptions made by those who advance the kinds of arguments outlined above.

The significance of such models for comprehending and explaining social phenomena has received a good deal of attention from philosophers of the social sciences. Behaviourist and cognitive-developmentalist paradigms in psychology have been identified with opposing models of man as passive respondent and initiator of action respectively, while sociologists are traditionally classified as 'systems' and 'action' theorists according to the emphasis they give to freewill and social determinism. One attempt to explain the development of opposing models of man and society has been particularly influential. This is Alan Dawe's theory of 'The two sociologies' (Dawe, 1971).

Dawe argues that there is not one sociology, but *two*, and that these are a result of two distinct responses to certain historical events: the enlightenment, the French revolution and the industrial revolution. The conservative reaction to the 'subversive rationalism' of the first, the 'traumatic disorder' of the second, and the 'destructive egoism' of the third, was to promote the case for order created by external social constraints. The problem of social disintegration was conceived as a consequence of Hobbes' pessimistic view of man as self-seeking to the point of mutual destruction unless individual actions are constrained by some strong moral authority. In the sociology of Durkheim this authority was in and of the social organism, in the form of the *conscience collective*. In the systems perspective of the later structural functionalists, socialization into the consensus of the central value system and the resultant norm-regulated behaviour were the means by which conformity was assured. Societal mechanisms for the treatment or correction of deviance function to 'mop up' the exceptions to the rule.

The radical reaction to these historical events leads to an emphasis on the contrasting concept of *control*. The Enlightenment with its libertarian and individualistic assertions of personal autonomy, entailed demands for release from the bondage of social ties and the liberation of the mind from 'fettering conditions'. Here the implicit model of man is an optimistic one. Obviously inspired by Rousseau's 'noble savage' and subsequently informed by the concept of 'alienation' in Marxist theory, man's potential for altruistic, cooperative and humane endeavour is considered to have been stunted by historical situations and repressive social institutions over which man has lost control. Neo-Marxist, 'action' and 'interpretive' sociologists are seen as the intellectual and methodological heirs of this tradition.

In the context of counselling theory, Daubner (1982) has outlined four theories of 'moral nature' and from them has inferred a variety of counsellor-perspectives which might be adopted. Fundamental to such perspectives will be the counsellor's explicit or implicit beliefs about 'the basic propensity of human beings when they make moral choices . . . Do they have a predisposition toward choosing the good, or the evil, or are they as likely to opt for the one as the other? Are they innately impelled by the good, by the evil, or are they originally neutral toward both?' (p. 180). Daubner suggests that the Rousseauian concept of the 'noble savage' epitomizes the 'theory of natural goodness', and the link with Marx is made through the attribution of avarice, ambition and evil in man to 'the institution of private property' (p. 181).

The antithesis of this model he identifies with strict Calvinist beliefs about original sin in which, in choosing evil over good, 'the first humans lost their original state of integrity and fell into a condition of complete corruption and depravity' (p. 184). The hopelessness of such a model is perceived in man's redemption being entirely in the hands of God: only the 'chosen', the 'elect', will be saved and then through God's choice and not through their own endeavours. Remove the theology, says Daubner, and you have something like Freud's model of man in which the rational and the social can at best only modify the 'destructive, antisocial, anticultural tendencies in all persons . . .' (p. 187).

Between these extremes, Daubner poses two further theories, those of 'neutrality' and 'deprivation'. According to the former, man is neither predisposed towards good or evil; rather he has 'the potentiality for both' (p. 189). Which, as a matter of fact, dominates an individual's course of action is a consequence of *learning*. In this model, man has no innate or 'built-in objectives' (p. 190), for goals are just as much learned as are the means by which they are sought.

According to the theory of Deprivation, it is in the nature of Man that through intellect and will — that is rationality — choices can be made between courses of action that are either 'good' or 'bad', and that a considerable tension between the rational and the emotions is a natural condition. In this version of 'original sin', man still has the potential to choose good over evil through the exercise of intellect, but in having chosen evil the first humans lost their 'original innocence', and thus made the exercise of that capacity so much harder for their descendents (p. 191–3). As Daubner summarizes:

> Whereas the theory of natural goodness emphasises the importance of original human nature unaided by any divine help, and Calvin's theory of total depravity stresses the complete ineptness of fallen human nature and the absolute negation of meritorious human effort, the theory of deprivation accents the fact that diminished human nature is aided and augmented by divine assistance.

If we now return to the four perspectives on the welfare state, we can see the degree to which these models of human nature are implicit in them. The Marxists have most clearly embraced the 'theory of natural goodness'. Engels' *Origins of the Family, Private Property and the State* is strongly reminiscent of Rousseau. His thesis is that the altruistic collective endeavours of 'primitive communism' are lost in the emergence of private property and the right of inheritance and the growth of the repressive state which protects the established order. Under communism, man could again be 'noble' and the state no longer necessary (thus 'withering away'), but first a revolution is required to throw off 'the fetters' of the existing social relations of production. Because nothing less than revolution can alter the basis of poverty, ignorance and alienation, man's realization of his potential for good is going to be quite strictly limited in the creation of welfare services of one kind or another. At best these will ameliorate the worst excesses of the system; at worst, they will represent subtle and insidious forms of social control.

The Anti-Collectivists, by contrast, are most at home with a systems sociology which stresses the self-adjustment of structures and functions in a natural strain towards equilibrium. Free enterprise economics is, after all, premised upon precisely such notions embodied in the 'laws' of supply and demand and the operation of the price mechanism. The model of 'economic man' who seeks only to enhance his personal satisfaction through maximizing profits and minimizing losses is a natural ingredient of such a theory, and in accepting the profit motive as the guiding principle, the Anti-Collectivists are accepting a model of man as naturally selfish. Indeed, the best thing to do is recognize that this is what 'human nature' is, and build a society upon it. The individual will most adequately serve society's needs by serving his *own*. While publicly rejecting the idea of 'complete corruption and depravity', Anti-Collectivists implicitly accept the impossibility of changing 'human nature' and in emphasizing the natural inequality of individuals also accept the inevitability of social progress via the talents of a élite. The Victorian conceptions of 'the rich man in his castle, the poor man at his gate' may no longer be so readily accepted, even by this group, but in effect their intolerance of state intervention in determining the standards of living of the individual is a consequence of their commitment to 'the natural order of things'. Where intervention *is* justified is in the control of the masses for the defence of the freedom of the élite to serve the 'common good' through its pursuit of personal gain. Effective socialization and societal sanctions for deviance are required to control man's potential for evil and divert his energies into socially acceptable forms of production and competition.

The Reluctant Collectivists also see man somewhat pessimistically. Recognizing that free-enterprise economy is neither totally efficient nor entirely just, and convinced that some men, at least, are naturally weak, this group will countenance institutionalized care where neither charity nor the market system meets reasonable human needs. It is perhaps to this perspective that Daubner's 'theory of neutrality' most applies. Man is neither predisposed to good nor to evil; rather those are propensities which are learned. Indeed, the Reluctant Collectivists consider themselves to be among the enlightened in perceiving both the limitations of capitalism and the higher-order priorities of justice and human need. They also perceive the weaknesses of their fellow-men, and their reluctant intervention is also justified as an act of benevolence towards those less fortunate than themselves. In attitude to man and in prescriptions for action, the Reluctant Collectivist is finally paternalistic with more than a hint about him of the sanctimony of the nineteenth century charity worker: 'There but for Grace of God go I. Fortunately *I* received the Grace ...'

With the Fabian Socialists, however, the balance swings towards the potential of Man for good. It is at least a happy coincidence that Daubner chooses the concept of 'deprivation' to label his third model, for it equates nicely with the socialists' conern for the cultural, social and material deprivation which makes equality of opportunity such an important (and elusive) goal. After centuries of capitalism, it is no longer easy for man to seek the 'good' rather than to serve self-interest, but that is not to say that it is impossible. The 'good' can be enhanced, not by the paternalistic salvation of the weak by the strong, but the creating of facilitatory structures in which *all* men may share the opportunities which life provides. Unfortunately, men are *not*, in fact equal — and it would be folly to imagine that they are — but they deserve equal consideration and at least a fair competition within which all may realize their (albeit unequal) potentials. Man is thus considered more positively than by those who view the welfare state with either fear or resignation but it is by no means the full-blown optimism of a Marx or a Rousseau.

Section 3:   Pastoral Care in Education

If we turn now to a consideration of education we may see how the thought, practice, and consideration of pastoral care relate to fundamental assumptions about the nature of man and attitudes to organized welfare provision. The picture is far from clear because it is difficult to separate influences on pastoral care from the complex combination of factors which have shaped education as a whole, and also because theorizing about pastoral care is at such an early stage of development that inconsistencies and internal contradictions abound. This is perhaps exemplified in what has become a standard assertion in the literature of pastoral care that you cannot separate the pastoral from the academic. If the latter were true there could not even be the literature in which it is proclaimed!

The picture is further clouded by responses to the competing demands of the practical situations which daily confront teachers and educational managers, and the desire to develop prescriptions for an educational world which, as yet, does not exist. Those who venture into print in this area find themselves struggling to advance their thinking about pastoral care as a positive contribution to welfare, only to be constantly reminded in their daily work that schools are more or less of a jungle in which the maintenance of discipline and a preoccupation with the transmission of pre-packaged knowledge give such a project a disconcerting air of unreality.

It is not surprising, therefore, that any attempt to classify the perspectives of individuals under either the four positions on the collective provision of welfare discussed in section one, or the four concepts of human nature discussed in the second section, is likely to fail. However, we suggest that a clearer understanding of the conventional wisdom of pastoral care can be achieved by looking at the degree to which the sentiments of the former and the assumptions of the latter are present in the thought and literature available. Their presence will have a dual significance; on the one hand these sentiments and assumptions may have directly influenced thought, while on the other they may be implied as a by-product of practitioners' attempts to legitimate their pragmatic reactions to daily pressures.

Examples of the influence of an Anti-Collectivist perspective employing a pessimistic model of man's moral nature are understandably difficult to find in the literature of pastoral care. This is because the preoccupations of the most conservative of educationalists are those which Skilbeck (1976, pp. 40–1) has summarized as:

> . . . clear and firm discipline, high attainment in examinations, continuity between past and present, the cohesion and orderly development of institutions and of the myths and rituals engendered by these institutions, . . . (and) . . . has been with predefined views about what it is fitting to do, feel, think and with standards of performance in all spheres. Education may be active but is always primarily an assimilative process: induction into institutions, acceptance of defined values and standards; initiation into clearly articulated modes of thought and action.

In such a perspective pastoral care as conventionally conceived either has no place or is translated into an alternative vocabulary of initiation and control. Thus, if one looks at the Black Papers, for example, it is difficult to identify any explicit position on pastoral care, guidance and counselling. One may, however, infer such a position from the kinds of things the Black Paper authors write about instead. Given this preoccupation with traditional culture, academic standards, obedience and the creation of élites, pastoral care could only ever be a form of oiling the machine, a means of facilitating the selection and differentiation of groups for initiation into Bantock's two curricula (Bantock 1968).

No doubt one could find examples of such a perspective in any staffroom. The hardbitten campaigner who sneers at pastoral care as 'cuddle therapy', the ineffective tutor whose problems of classroom control dominate his perspective such that pastoral care (and indeed everything else!) reduce to his need for disciplinary back-up (Best *et al.* 1983, pp. 74–5) and the sixth-form specialist who sees pastoral care as either irrelevant or a distraction from the pursuit of academic excellence, are all either implicitly or explicitly adopting and confirming such a perspective. Theirs is the world of black and white, of good and bad, of valuable and valueless, where the 'Good' is identified with the traditional and hierarchical concepts of knowledge and learning.

Such views are, of course, the targets for educationalists who operate somewhere near the other end of the spectrum. Again, writings by Marxists, progressivists, libertarians and the new romantics make few references to the concept of pastoral care, because their preoccupations are such that the concept is simply inappropriate. For them, it is about neither the 'pastoral' nor the 'academic' (let alone the dubious relationship between the two), but about 'education'. The thrust of their arguments is that whatever may go on in schools under either label is *not* education but something else: 'schooling'. This kind of perspective is summed up by John Holt (1977), who says:

> Education, with its supporting system of compulsory and competitive schooling, all its carrots and sticks, its grades, diplomas and credentials, now seems to me perhaps the most authoritarian and dangerous of all social inventions of mankind. It is the deepest foundation of the modern and worldwide slave state, in which most people feel themselves to be nothing but producers, consumers, spectators and 'fans', driven more and more, in all parts of their lives by greed, envy and fear. My concern is not to improve 'education' but to do away with it, to end the ugly and antihuman business of people-shaping and to allow and help people to shape themselves (p. 8).

Again, it is possible to infer the kind of perspective such writers must implicitly hold of pastoral care. It will tend to be seen on the one hand as what it ought to be and, on the other, what it is: it *ought* to be quite superfluous as a separate category, structure or practice since education is about the self-development of whole persons whose well-being cannot be so subdivided; it *is* a more or less subtle form of social control through the exacting of obedience and the dishonest manipulation and steering that passes for 'guidance and counselling'.

The person who comes nearest to advancing this view in the literature of pastoral care is Derek Williamson (1980). He argues that pastoral care systems in schools perform different functions in respect of different groups of pupils. Those who accept, and in some measure find relevant, the traditional academic curriculum and the rules of the scholastic game receive support and guidance in their academic pursuits. Those who rebel against an academic diet which is irrelevant and alienating are defined as 'problems' and referred to the pastoral system for treatment. The function the pastoral system performs in their case Williamson terms 'pastoralization': a delightful coining since like 'Pasteurisation' its purpose is to render material harmless! Pastoralization has been achieved when the dissidents have been persuaded to accept the academic status-quo. All this ultimately works against education, because it distracts attention from the basic inadequancy of the learning experiences which the mainstream of the curriculum offers. In effect the real failings of the system are concealed behind the pastoral smokescreen.

This position is very reminiscent of the Marxist apprehension about the desirability of a welfare state. For as long as welfare is seen as needed only by those who cannot cope in the mainstream of the economy, so the fundamental evils of the capitalist system will not be confronted. Neither will the nation as a whole or education in particular embrace a positive view of man in which welfare is not some kind of institutionalized charity but a positive contribution to the promotion of a new era in which the innate propensity for good in man is realizable. Again the optimistic assumptions of Daubner's 'theory of natural goodness' are clearly accepted by the Progressivists. As Holt (1977, p. 120) puts it:

> There is no way to find out how much good or kindness there may be in human nature, except to build or try to build a society on the assumption that people are or would like to be good and kind, a society in which to be good and kind is at least not a handicap.

It is in the middle ground between the conservatism of the Black Papers and the radical stand of Holt and Williamson that the majority of the literature on pastoral care may be located. The dominant strain of thought is most comfortably aligned with the Fabian Socialist picture of welfare and the concept of man as having at least as much of a predisposition towards good as towards evil, with the former perhaps suffering as a result of deprivation. For the Fabian Socialists, the attack on deprivation is an important means of liberating man's potential for good, although this is often seen as change within a system rather than a challenge to it. Further, this is held to be achievable through a combination of planning and individual liberty in the form of appropriate institutions and organizational arrangements.

The seminal work of Marland (1974) translates these views quite precisely into a case for pastoral care in education: 'it really is a truism of school planning that what you want to happen must be institutionalized. It is not enough to rely on goodwill, dedication, hard work, personality and so on . . .' (p. 11).

Marland applies the deprivation thesis quite specifically when he portrays pastoral care as a means by which schools might increase their power in mitigating the effects of extra-school factors (p. 7). Marland accepts the relationship between deprivation and the concept of equality of opportunity and sees pastoral care as in part an institutionalized response to the problem. But he does not do so simply as a reluctant collectivist accepts some welfare services as a necessary net to catch the inadequate. Pastoral care is more than a way of coping: it is part of the central educational purpose of schooling in its positive promotion of growth and development. However, Marland's influential volume exhibits the weaknesses of an early attempt to grapple with the tensions between theoretical prescriptions and harsh realities; there are inconsistencies and uncertainties in it, many of which have not been resolved in later works. Marland and his contributors seem undecided as to whether pastoral care is the central task of the school or a lubricant for its educational function, conventionally conceived; or whether pastoral care is concerned with the total welfare of all children (p. 17), as a way of seeking 'the wider completing of the process of meeting pupils' needs' (p. 5), or a means of either compensating or complementing the environment of a section of the school population (p. 24). When implied as a right of *all* children, pastoral care seems to endorse Daunt's (1975) 'equal value principle' yet as a facilitator of equality of opportunity the competitive principle is presumed. In the context of the latter, Marland is capable of a paternalism which may be found in the least radical of the Fabians as much as in the Reluctant Collectivists. At its worst, he might be accused of a certain smugness in his assertion that 'a school must be able to offer guidance without dictation, advice without domination, and a firm framework for growth. Above all it must know its pupils closely enough to be able to relate to them' (p. 46).

Even those who have entered the arena as critics of the conventional wisdom of pastoral care seem to end up advocating courses of action which are limited in scope and scale. The 1977 paper by Best *et al.* has sometimes been cited as a turning-point in pastoral care theory because it was the first publication to advance a systematic critique of the conventional wisdom of Marland (1974), Haigh (1975) *et al.* However, the collection of readings the authors subsequently produced (Best *et al.* 1980), while extending this critique in various ways, is primarily an attempt to bring reality closer to the rhetoric within schools whose basic structures and functions are not finally challenged. Their programmes for change (p. 276–9) are Fabian: more effective evaluation of practice, better and more integrated structures of roles, clearer curriculum planning, developing expert services and so on. Schools as we know them are not challenged. Rather the point is to make them better places through planned and gradual reforms of modest proportions.

This is a position which the same team take up in the final chapter of their subsequent research report (Best *et al.* 1983). In a chapter significantly titled 'Getting it right', their conclusions are presented as a set of prescriptions for a school seeking to improve its pastoral provision without threatening the schools' right to go on existing in a fundamentally unchanged form. This position is characteristic of other similar works: McGuiness (1982) *Planned Pastoral Care*, Johnson *et al.* (1980) *Secondary Schools and the Welfare Network*, Blackham (1978) *Education for Personal Autonomy*, and the majority of the contributions to the journal *Pastoral Care in Education*. As with earlier writers, it may well be that these authors have all stopped short of a commitment to a full-blooded Marxism or Progressivism embracing a model of man deified, because they are daily involved as teachers in situations in which pragmatic responses seem to make such a position untenable. Further, all are involved in schooling and it is neither wise nor easy to set about demolishing the source of one's subsistence!

Some authors have been even less clear about their view of man and thus of the nature and functions of pastoral care. Douglas Hamblin is a striking case in point. In his book *The Teacher and Pastoral Care* (1978), he asserts that 'the primary task of the pastoral team is to develop an environment which adapts to the needs of pupils of all abilities and backgrounds' (p. xv), a child-centred position which is developed later in the book in regard to self-assessment, self-image, personal development programmes and so on. However, the model of man as free and autonomous disappears from view when such problems as aggressive behaviour are confronted. In a later article, (Hamblin, 1980) the problem of disruptive classes is attacked through a mixture of group 'guidance' and behaviour modification in which a behaviourist view of man is employed in advocating what are essentially means of control.

Hamblin's writings are highly thought of by many practitioners not least because they seem to offer practical solutions to pressing problems, and any contributions to such a long neglected issue as pastoral care are obviously to be welcomed. However, there must be doubts about the soundness in practice of an eclecticism which appears to combine concepts and procedures which are inherently at odds with one another. This is a charge which can be levelled at the practitioner-oriented literature of pastoral care generally: the overwhelming impression is one of a realistic pragmatism which quite ignores the profound differences which exist in conceptions of man, society and schooling which we have been at pains to highlight.

Conclusion

It is all too easy in education as in politics to make much of issues which represent relatively minor differences in positions which are publicly adopted while ignoring the deeper conflicts which underlie them. In the process, the degree of consensus which exists is all too easily exaggerated and appeals to 'common sense', 'what any reasonable person would agree' or popular opinion are made all the more plausible. Everyone might agree that 'pastoral care', like 'welfare', is 'a good thing' in some abstract sense, but we have tried to show in this paper that attitudes to both as institutionalized social structures are diverse and cover the whole spectrum from wholehearted support to violent opposition.

The significance of this conflict can be seen to derive in part from the fundamentally different assumptions that are made about the nature of man as a moral, social and political being, and in part from the greater or lesser commitment of the protagonists to the political and educational status quo. No amount of hard-headed pragmatism or convenient eclecticism can resolve these fundamental differences, nor alter the fact that to adopt a position on pastoral care in education is as much a deeply moral and political act as to enter the arena of debate on the desirability of the welfare state.

The evolving conventional wisdom of pastoral care has yet to include an awareness of the significance of these issues. Some have been content to seek 'practical solutions to practical problems' on a day-to-day basis, while others have begun to explore the potential of planned pastoral care in, for example, tutorial work programmes. Others have engaged in theoretical debate about the finer distinctions between the concepts involved. And yet others have begun to develop critiques of the conventional wisdom itself. None, it seems to us, have gone very far in contextualizing their work in the framework of political and social models which exist. As with attitudes to the welfare state, most seem to end up somewhere in the middle ground with the literature predominantly Fabian in direction.

What must be questioned is whether this is enough. Are we to settle for the development and refining of a dimension of schooling which is perhaps a means for the conservation of an overt curriculum whose value for many children is difficult to justify, and a hidden curriculum dominated by a model of the child which is quite opposed to the educational ideal of rational and moral autonomy? Or are we to hold out for a radical and fundamental change in what schools stand for such that they become forces for progress and emancipation in which pastoral care with all its implications as a paternalistic supplement to the mainstream of schooling becomes simply irrelevant?

These are weighty questions indeed. To provide an answer is no less than a wager on the nature of man.

The Welfare Curriculum and the Work of the School

Peter Ribbins
University of Birmingham

Meeting the Needs of Pupils

For schools, the needs of pupils should be paramount. Few would contest such a claim but what it actually entails is less clear. In thinking about the needs of the individual pupil I find it helpful to make distinctions between those needs which:

1   *All* pupils have for education for cognitive development;
2   *All* pupils have for education for affective, moral, social and personal development;
3   *All* pupils have for general welfare and order;
4   *Some* pupils have for emotional, social and educational support and encouragement as they encounter particular personal problems which tax them to the limit and beyond.

How effectively do schools meet these needs?

My interest in this chapter is essentially with the second of the needs listed above and with the ways in which schools have responded to it. One thing at least seems clear. Over the last few years education for Personal, Social and Moral Development (PSM) has been 'rediscovered' or has, at least, experienced something of a renaissance. This, despite the fact that 'educators have been concerned about the personal, social and moral development of their charges since the time of Moses' (Wakeman, 1984, p. 10) and that 'schools have always been concerned with personal and social development' (Pring, 1984, p. 2). What then is new?

Three things at least. The first has to do with the *origins* of the revival of interest identified above. The second turns upon developments in our thinking about the *meaning* and significance of education in this area and the third is concerned with changing views as to the *means* of its delivery within schools and colleges. Much of the rest of this chapter will deal briefly with each of these three issues and with an analysis of the extent to which their interaction has led to demands for the implementation of what I shall term as a 'Welfare Curriculum' within the contemporary secondary school.

Why the Renewed Interest in Education for Personal Social and Moral Development?

The fact of renewed interest is easy enough to document. It can be seen in developments in the institutional practices of schools over the last decade. As David (1982) remarks, 'In recent years secondary schools have developed measures to enhance the personal and social development of their students, through the operation of the pastoral care system and through developments in the curriculum. These measures take many forms and are often fragmented . . . ' (p. 7). It can also be seen in a growing concern with this issue in official and quasi-official circles as expressed in a number of reports and statements (APU, 1980; DES, 1979, 1981; HMI, 1979, 1980; Schools Council, 1981) which have, as Pring (1984) puts it 'usually expressed the view that personal and social development needs a more centralized and explicit place in the curriculum' (p. 2).

Criticisms of this aspect of the activities of schools are usually discretely encoded in such official reports, but other commentators have been less reserved:

> Changes in the school curriculum are being outpaced by changes in society . . . this gap has now reached such critical proportions that it challenges the legitimacy of the content and method of the curriculum in schools today . . . The value system of schooling has been predominantly linguistically, cognitively and intellectually based with little emphasis on the emotional, intuitive, practical and experiential aspects of human development (Baldwin and Smith, 1983, p. 40).

To an extent, HMI appear to share this view. Thus they have argued that 'The personal and social development of the pupil is one way of describing the central purpose of education' (HMI, 1979, p. 206) and that, as such, it, 'ought to represent a major charge on the curriculum' (HMI, 1980, p. 2). But does it? In a survey which focused upon the provision made for fourth and fifth forms in a sample of 384 secondary schools HMI (1979) concluded that:

> in general, schools placed much greater emphasis on fostering the personal development of their pupils through pastoral care than through their curriculum. In only a seventh of schools of all types did HMI consider that sufficient detailed attention had been given to the ways in which the curriculum could serve the pupils' needs in this broader sense (p. 208).

By the time this was written, thinking about the pastoral dimension of schooling was already beginning to shift away from an exclusive concern 'with providing individual guidance to pupils as they passed through the system and with mopping up the casualties so that they could return to the fray' to one which laid much greater stress on 'involving pupils in a range of learning processes within groups designed to enable them to cope more effectively' (Blackburn, 1983b, p. 20). As Marland (1980), in a seminal paper, put it:

> *the art of the pastoral system is to help all the individuals without always giving individual help* ... The most effective individual guidance and counselling depends on the background of concepts, facts and skills which the individual client brings to the counselling session ... individual counselling has to depend on whole-group exploration of this necessary background. Drawing up the list of what should go into that background is essentially a curriculum matter. The curriculum components which relate especially to individual and personal growth I would call the 'pastoral curriculum' (pp. 153, 154).

Debates on the kinds of issues identified above have been more than a little confused by a lack of clear and shared usage of the terms employed and to some conflict as to the meanings which ought to be attached to the crucial concepts involved. Since much of the confusion is related to superficial differences in usage rather than to fundamental conflicts at the level of conceptualization, some clarification should be possible. Such a clarification may well begin by looking for the right questions to ask. These might properly include some of the following. What is meant by the idea of giving the curriculum a pastoral dimension? To what extent does such a development entail a pastoral curriculum? What is meant by the notion of a 'pastoral curriculum' and other similar concepts? How do such activities relate to and how are they derived from the purposes of the more fundamental dimensions of schooling?

Giving the Curriculum a Pastoral Flavour

If the idea that the curriculum should be given a pastoral flavour has become fashionable in educational circles and if terms such as 'pastoral curriculum' have become commonplace in the everyday language of a wide variety of people involved in education, this should not be taken to imply either that clear and shared understandings exist as to the meanings which ought to be attached to such concepts or that the values, structures or practices they may be taken to entail, have gone unchallenged. Thus, for example, a senior HMI has commented that 'in welcoming a wider view of curriculum objectives we don't want to substitute for an older pastoral-academic divide a newer division, this time within the curriculum itself, between the cognitive and the caring' (Lord, 1983, p. 10). A view, it seems, which may well be shared by many teachers. Ribbins and Ribbins (1984), reporting on the development of a PSM programme in a comprehensive school in the South-West, encountered teachers who questioned whether schools or teachers ought to be deeply involved in 'pastoral care', let alone in the teaching of a pastoral curriculum. As one remarked 'Our aim must be orientated towards education rather than in trying to right all the ills of society' and another made the point that 'a teacher should be a teacher. An adult with a mastery of his subject and a trained skill in imparting it. That surely is a sufficient contribution to society — more is self deluding folly'. A senior member of staff echoes a reservation, in some ways similar to that expressed by Lord (1983) quoted above: 'There is a need for a pastoral aspect of the curriculum but not for a pastoral curriculum, although we may call it that — and perhaps thereby encourage the advent of the great curriculum divide.'

Recently, a number of philosophers of education have turned their attention upon such concepts as 'Education for PSM Development', 'The Pastoral Curriculum' and the like. Their interest if somewhat belated is much to be welcomed. As Pring (1984) has argued:

> The difficulties are to some extent philosophical. In clarifying ideas on personal and social development for curriculum purposes, one is quickly into issues about which philosophers

have a lot to say — for example, what it is to be a person ...,
the relation of personal rights and responsibilities to the social
good. Not to see these problems for what they are — the
subject matter at a certain level of analysis, of ethics, of the
philosophy of mind, of political and social philosophy —
would be to trivialize them, and ultimately to trivialize the
curriculum thinking in this area (p. 8).

None of this should be taken to imply that philosophers, any
more than, say, economists, necessarily agree with one another. On
the contrary they do often disagree and this can be illustrated by
examining the debates on the notion of the 'Pastoral Curriculum'
which have been taking place over the last two or three years between
Elliott (1983), Hibberd (1984) and Mclaughlin (1982, 1983).

In thinking about the notion of the 'pastoral curriculum' a major
problem lies in the fact that it is used in a variety of more or less
different ways. It may be useful to think of a continuum of usage
with towards one polar extreme what might be described as an
encompassing conception in which would be included 'all the curriculum
work undertaken by the school in the area of personal and social
education — moral education, health education, sex education and so
on' (Mclaughlin, 1983, p. 92). Towards the other polar extreme
would be a much more *restrictive* usage of the term 'to refer to work
more closely associated with pastoral care' (*Ibid*). Quite frequently,
those who have considered the concept of the 'pastoral curriculum'
slip rather indiscriminately from one such kind of usage to the other,
often in the context of the same paper.

Marland (1980), for example, seems to adopt both approaches
simultaneously. Thus on the one hand he describes the 'pastoral
curriculum' as 'The curriculum components which relate especially to
individual and personal growth' (p. 154) and argues that the aim of
such a curriculum should be to establish the background of concepts,
facts and skills which the individual needs. Mclaughlin (1982) objects
to this definition on the grounds that it is excessively general and
vague and, more importantly, entails an unnecessary confusion with
the notion of *'liberal education'*.

I shall return to this last issue shortly. At this point let us attempt
to clarify what Mclaughlin (1982) regards as a more acceptable
definition of the 'Pastoral Curriculum' based upon what I have
described as a *restrictive* use of the term. In developing this view,
Mclaughlin turns to what he identifies as Marland's (1980) own more
refined and restrictive usage:

> Marland begins to be more precise in his outline of the notion
> of the 'pastoral curriculum' when he writes that it is con-
> cerned solely with 'the personal needs of the pupil resolving
> his individual problems, making informed decisions and
> taking his place in his personal and social world' and that any
> item of content in this area should be determined by what is
> — 'essential for the personal growth of individuals, for their
> learning growth ... not ... because it is part of the logic of a
> subject' (p. 36).

This being so, the aim of this part of the curriculum, Mclaughlin
argues, is clearly specific, instrumental and utilitarian in character. As
I have pointed out, his essential objection to wider definitions of the
concept of the 'pastoral curriculum' is that they entail unnecessary
confusion with that of 'liberal education'. What are we to make of
this claim?

One problem is that Mclaughlin does not have a lot to say about
'liberal education' in the first of his two papers and even less in the
second. He does claim that:

> One of the major elements of the curriculum is in my view
> concerned with 'liberal education'. Now no one clear sense
> can be attached to this notion nor can it be regarded as
> unproblematic in itself. For purposes of this paper, however,
> it might be valuable to employ a rather crude characterization
> of Liberal Education which lays particular emphasis on two
> features commonly stressed in accounts of the notion viz:
> *Generality* and Non-instrumentality (Mclaughlin, 1982,
> p. 37).

The merit of such a procedure, he claims, lies in its value in
'sharpening up our attention on the distinctive features of the
"pastoral curriculum"'. But he does also recognize that 'leaving
unexamined the central notion of "Liberal Education" may perhaps
lead to the making of distinctions between the various elements of the
curriculum which are oversimplified' (*ibid*). In fact Mclaughlin makes
a number of attempts to say what he means by the notion of 'Liberal
Education', perhaps the most interesting of which questions Marland's wider view of the pastoral curriculum which stresses the
contribution it might make to the personal needs and growth of the
individual:

> Is not Liberal Education — the broad and non-instrumental
> initiation of the pupil into the various domains of knowledge

— also related to 'individual and personal growth?' ... And are not the concepts, attitudes, facts and skills developed in Liberal Education also 'necessary to the individual' *in some sense*? (p. 36, writer's italics).

Now Mclaughlin does not make it clear what he means by the idea that Liberal Education may be 'necessary to the individual'. Taken at face value this appears to be just the kind of instrumental justification that he is at some pains to reject elsewhere. In the second of his papers this idea is not repeated and the author returns to what might be characterized as 'classic' and, perhaps, 'safer' justifications in which:

Liberal education is *general* in the sense that there is an attempt to introduce pupils into the range of different kinds of knowledge so they become aware of the breadth and scope of that knowledge. It is *non-instrumental* in the sense that the aim is not thereby to help directly individuals to face any particular problems they may be confronted with, but to develop understanding (Mclaughlin, 1983, p. 93).

Elliott (1982), whilst accepting much of such an analysis questions whether:

The development of capacities for practical judgment is ... a separate and independent process from the development of understanding through the various forms of knowledge (p. 54).

And suggests that:

It is on the basis of his assumption that the development of capacities for understanding can be logically separated from capacities for practical judgment, that Mclaughlin feels able to demarcate a distinctively 'pastoral curriculum' (*ibid*).

Elliott rejects this and argues that 'In my view, the capacity for knowledge and understanding does not develop independently of the capacity for practical judgment' and suggests that the 'fact that many pupils in schools do not grasp the practical relevance of what they are taught indicates a deficiency in the quality of teaching' (*ibid*). He also argues that the development of 'pastoral curricular' in schools outside the mainstream curriculum 'is a tacit admission that the latter is failing to provide pupils with a truly liberal education; an education which is both intellectually challenging and personally significant for the way they live their lives' (*ibid*).

Finally, Elliott points out that in:

> logically separating a practically orientated 'pastoral curriculum' from a mainstream liberal education which aims at developing 'knowledge and understanding', Mclaughlin inevitably gives the former lower status (p. 55).

Whereas 'I want to redefine the idea of the "pastoral curriculum" so that it becomes an integral part of the liberal education we ought to be offering pupils in schools' (*ibid*). Such a scenario has much in common with one of the central tenets of the 'conventional wisdom' of pastoral care (see Best *et al.*, 1983) given Elliott's claim that 'rather than being a subordinate consideration, "the pastoral curriculum" ought to have an over-riding importance in curriculum planning for a liberal education' (p. 55).

These are serious criticisms and Mclaughlin (1983) has made some attempt to answer them. Elliott, Mclaughlin argues, has misunderstood what he was trying to say; 'I am not claiming that the various elements of the whole school curriculum *are* totally separate from each other. For example I am not suggesting that the liberal education element of the curriculum has *no bearing* upon the practical kinds of decisions and adjustments that I have argued to be the particular concern of the pastoral curriculum' (p. 94). He acknowledges that: 'An adequate school curriculum must contain elements which vary in terms of their *direct relevance* to the rather practical aspects of "preparation for life" (*ibid*). And that:

> The pastoral curriculum *is* precisely concerned in my view with these aspects. Although it is clearly related — and must be related — to liberal education, this latter element through its provision of a wide background of knowledge and understanding only *indirectly* — and at a very different level — contributes to the kind of 'preparation for life' which is the particular concern of the pastoral curriculum (*ibid*).

If Mclaughlin still seems committed to the view that the 'pastoral curriculum' ought to be conceived of as essentially detailed, specific and instrumental, he may have softened his earlier view that it should focus 'fairly hard on equipping the pupil to make practical decisions, judgments and adjustments for themselves and their own lives' (Mclaughlin, 1982, p. 42).

Taken as a whole, the debate between Mclaughlin and Elliott has undoubtedly identified many of the key problems in thinking about the 'pastoral curriculum' and its relationship with other aspects of the school curriculum. Much at issue between them turns upon competing conceptions as to what meanings could be given to the central concept of 'liberal education' and to its implicatios for the purposes and practices of the school curriculum. However, neither author explores the concept of 'liberal education' in any depth. This is not to suggest that either Mclaughlin or Elliott have claimed to do so. On the contrary, the former openly acknowledges that he has left the concept 'largely' unexamined and expresses the hope that 'subsequent discussion' may lead to a 'fuller exploration' of the relevant issues. Such a 'fuller exploration' of the notion of 'liberal education' and its implications for the notion of the 'pastoral curriculum' is beyond the scope of this paper. But, whoever takes it on in the future will at least be able to make use of Bailey's (1984) recently published and most useful examination of liberal education in *Beyond the Present and the Particular*. We should, however, try to be clear about what such an analysis can and can not do. It can make us clearer about the 'pastoral curriculum' as an aspect of the curriculum dimension of schooling. But the curriculum dimension, however important, is only one aspect of the school and if we are to relate such ideas as the pastoral curriculum to schooling as a whole we will need to take account of such other dimensions as those concerned with welfare, order and administration as well. It is the main purpose of this paper to make a preliminary attempt at such an analysis. Before turning to this, there are a few further distinctions between the 'pastoral curriculum' and other aspects of the curriculum which I shall need to discuss.

If it is a special concern with the practical needs of the individual which, for Mclaughlin (1983), distinguishes the 'pastoral curriculum' from the purposes of 'liberal education' it also serves to differentiate it from yet another curriculum area which he terms the 'academic curriculum', 'where this is seen as the detailed and systematic study of a particular discipline aiming at the preparation of the students to become specialists (in some sense) in that discipline' (p. 93). Two further distinctions seem worth making.

In the first of these Mclaughlin (1982) distinguishes between 'the pastoral curriculum' and those other aspects of schooling which are concerned with education for PSM development. This distinction seems to entail something of a paradox. On the one hand 'the scope of the pastoral curriculum is potentially unlimited' (p. 39) to the extent that even a specific approach such as ATW spans 'diverse areas such as adjustment to life in school, developing study skills ... general social development, coping with specific aspects of life such as relations with others, health, sex, moral decisions and so on' (p. 40),

yet 'I am not suggesting that the term "pastoral curriculum" ...
covers *all* the curriculum components concerned with Social and
Personal Education. In my view the "pastoral curriculum" is only
part of this broader area' (p. 39). In offering such a stipulative
definition of the notion of a 'pastoral curriculum', Mclaughlin seems
to be distinguishing between two forms of personal and social
education. One of which entails 'a kind of equipping of the child with
a basic set of knowledge and skills necessary for survival in our
society ...' (p. 44) and, as such, has come to be termed the 'pastoral
curriculum'. But there is another aspect in which 'there is no
immediate stress on the rather utilitarian preparation I have associated with the "Pastoral Curriculum"' and in which the kind of basic
preparation discussed above is 'not adequate as an approach to what
could justifiably be called "Education" in this area' (*ibid*). Now this
is not to denigrate the first of these aspects of personal and social
education. On the contrary: 'It is *important*, something *currently
neglected*; something *worth doing*; but it is not *enough* in this area.
The "Pastoral Curriculum" is necessary but not sufficient' (p. 44).
What is needed is:

> That the whole curriculum is closely looked at from the
> perspective of Social and Personal Education generally ...
> That with regard specifically to the 'Pastoral curriculum'
> there is a need to ensure that the material being covered is
> linked in with the co-ordinated material outlined (above),
> particularly so that the depth and complexity of treatment in
> the background area can be brought to bear on the more
> specifically focused area (pp. 45, 46).

Other writers, such as David (1982) and Pring (1984), who have
focused mainly on education for PSM development appear to share
this view. In Pring's (1984) case this is hardly surprising. Because,
although his treatment of the place of PSM Education in the
curriculum is a major contribution to thinking on this issue, his
examination of the concept of the 'pastoral curriculum' is both brief
(less than four pages) and somewhat derivative. In distinguishing the
pastoral curriculum from other aspects of the activities of the school
designed to facilitate the personal growth of pupils he acknowledges
his debt to Mclaughlin's (1983) ideas in shaping his own thinking on
this theme (p. 149).

Finally, whatever the limitations of Pring's (1984) treatment of
the notion of the 'Pastoral Curriculum', he does point to at least two
further sets of distinctions which may be significant. In the first of

these, he emphasises the need for 'a more skilled and systematic approach to the role of personal tutor and to the period set aside for this work' (p. 150). In this 'lies the significance of Leslie Button's work (1974, 1980) and that of Baldwin and Wells (1979, 1980, 1981)' who have worked out a developmental group work approach designed to facilitate the socialization of the child and to enhance their personal growth. To achieve this 'The most obvious place for developmental group work as the central core of the "pastoral curriculum" is the tutorial period, although the teaching strategies and general orientation could with profit be extended into different curriculum areas' (p. 151). The differentiation entailed here is between that aspect of the pastoral curriculum which gives particular attention to the developmental needs of children as indentified above, and which is the proper preserve of the tutorial period and its associated tutorial programme, and the rest of the pastoral curriculum. That distinctions of this sort are to be found in the institutional practices of schools can be illustrated from the case of 'Deanswater' and in the words of the Head of Fourth Year and of Personal and Social Education:

> (It was decided that) a separate Social and Personal Development Programme ... was necessary ... this decision entailed ... that ... there would be something of a division of the pastoral curriculum. Thus the Design for Living Course would be concerned mainly with the social education of pupils in these years whilst tutorial period would deal more with their interpersonal, interactional ... etc. needs (Ribbins and Ribbins, 1984, p. 7).

Important as this distinction between the notion of the 'pastoral curriculum' and the 'tutorial programme' is, it is of less significance than another point which Pring (1984) makes in attempting to answer a question which asks 'How schools might go about promoting education for PSM development?'

> Two major tasks ... confront the school that intends to take seriously personal, social and moral education. First there are general questions that should be asked about the curriculum and the *life of the school as a whole*. Secondly, ... the school needs to consider how and where there needs to be specific teaching to ensure that the different aspects of personal, social and moral education ... can be analyzed (p. 87, my emphasis).

There are two warnings here, and they are both important.

The first of these stresses that it is a mistake to assume that a concern for the PSM development of young persons raise exclusively curriculum questions. Or that it entails putting,

> another subject,namely personal and social education into the time-table. It *might* be important to look at the content of the curriculum ... but ... there are more significant questions to be asked about the conditions of learning, the impact of the curriculum as a whole upon young people and the relationships between teacher and pupil (p. 92).

Crucial to this aspect of their development is the respect young people have of themselves and 'no amount of instruction in personal, social and moral development can compensate for the destruction of the dignity that the constant experience of failure brings to so many pupils. But to provide this sense of personal worth and competence requires not another subject but a way of approaching old subjects and of relating to young persons' (pp. 92, 93).

Other writers have made the same kind of point although the terms they use may differ somewhat. Bulman (1984) emphasizes that 'apart from time within the curriculum, whether tutorial or academic, the pupils receive much of their pastoral education through the "hidden" curriculum' (p. 108). Like Pring, she also stresses that, 'Above all the attitudes of all the personnel in the school to each other and to the pupils has an enormously important message for the pupils viz a viz the pastoral curriculum and its goals' (*ibid*). And, although it may be very difficult, 'any implementation of the pastoral curriculum must look ... at the organization of the school itself and analyze the ways the school is helping or hindering the aims of the pastoral curriculum ...' (p. 109). David (1982) adopts a similar stance, stressing that the 'aims of personal and social education are central to the aims of education in general. Differences between the aims and objectives of a school's personal and social education programme and those of the school as a whole could make it unlikely that either will be seen as relevant' (p. 19). For a particularly forceful articulation of this view we might turn to Sockett (1975) who concludes from his examination of *Aims and Objects in Social Education* that 'one can think of no greater recipe for chaos than a curriculum which celebrates autonomy and a school social structure which inhibits and diminishes it'.

If the first of Pring's warnings is that to focus undue attention on the curricular implications of a heightened concern for education for

PSM development is to run the risk of deflecting attention from other aspects of schooling which may also need to be changed, this should not be interpreted to mean that taking PSM education seriously does not or should not have curricular implications. On the contrary, a 'concern for the *context* of the curriculum should not be seen as an excuse for doing nothing about the formal, time-tabled curriculum itself' (p. 110).

Suggestions as to the objectives and content of a curriculum designed to foster the social, personal, moral and affective development of young people are to be found in a wide variety of texts. Thus several 'maps of the field' for education for PSM have been published (APU, 1980; David, 1982, Pring, 1984), and numerous 'frameworks', 'schemes', 'programmes' etc. have been proposed for a pastoral curriculum (Bulman, 1984, Marland, 1980, Mclaughlin, 1982) and for tutorial programmes of one kind or another (Baldwin and Wells, 1979, 1980, 1981; Button, 1981; Hopson and Scally, 1981). In many of these texts and in numerous others as well it is widely recognized that the implementation of such ambitious schemes and ideas entails curriculum planning at a variety of levels and a good deal of staff preparation and training. Important as these and many other issues are they will receive no further attention in this paper. Rather, I shall attempt to sketch out an analytical model designed to relate the various ideas and concepts about 'personal, social and moral education', 'the pastoral curriculum', 'tutorial programmes', etc. to each other and to the more fundamental dimensions of schooling. In developing this argument, I shall rely heavily on yet another concept — that of the 'welfare curriculum' — which has, thus far, received limited attention in the literature.

The Welfare Curriculum, and the Work of the School: A Model

The model takes as its point of departure the proposition that schools are engaged in a wide variety of activities which may be accounted for and justified in terms of the contribution which they make to *'the good'* of the child. The implications of this proposition have been discussed at some length elsewhere in terms of an analysis which seeks to relate the pastoral, academic and disciplinary dimensions of schooling to the good of the pupil conceived in terms of the contribution which they make to the welfare and education of the individual child and the maintenance of that irreducible minimum of order without which any kind of social life would be intolerable (see Best *et al.*, 1983; Best and Ribbins, 1983). A revised version of this analysis may assist us to sort out some of the issues raised earlier in this chapter. This is an argument which is probably best expressed diagramatically (see Figure 1).

Circle 1 represents those activities in which schools engage which have as their central purpose the development and betterment of the child as a pupil by transforming him or her through the medium of the curriculum into an 'educated person'. For many, this is seen as the central purpose of schooling. Area A represents that aspect of the curricular work of the school which is concerned exclusively with the cognitive or academic education of the child in the way in which these terms have been defined earlier in this chapter. However, there is another aspect of the curriculum which is concerned particularly with the education of pupils for social, moral, personal and affective development. For some writers this whole area of curriculum activity (X and Y) is synonymous with the concept of the 'pastoral curriculum'. Others take the view that this area of the curriculum is more appropriately described in the terms of education for personal, social and moral development with the notion of the pastoral curriculum being given a more restricted meaning. As Mclaughlin (1982), to some extent following Marland (1980), has argued, the notion of the 'pastoral curriculum' should be restricted to those things which focus 'fairly hard on equipping the pupils to make practical decisions, judgments and adjustments for themselves and their own lives' (p. 42).

In this latter conception it is proposed that education for personal, social and moral development has two aspects. The first is represented in Circle 1 as Area X and the second by Area Y. To some extent both are seen as sharing similar areas of concern, covering broadly the same kinds of topics but doing so in very different ways in which X represents an essentially 'educational' experience whilst Y is more concerned with meeting the practical needs of the individual (see Mclaughlin, 1982, p. 44). If, for Mclaughlin, it is a particular concern with meeting the practical needs of the individual which characterizes the 'pastoral curriculum', Marland (1980) stresses those needs which may be thought of 'as "personal", that is, those which underpin *pastoral care*' (p. 158).

In a sense, then, the notion of the 'pastoral curriculum' may be said to entail both an educational purpose (albeit, perhaps, a somewhat restricted one) and a pastoral purpose. If the education of the child is conceived of as one expression of the commitment of the

Figure 1:   Relating the Different Aspects of the Welfare Curriculum to Each
Other and to the Primary Dimensions of Schooling

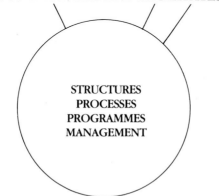

3. (DISCIPLINARY) ORDER

C
Oriented towards an
orderly social
collectivity

B
Oriented
towards the
needs of
the child
as a
person
and an
individ-
ual

A
Oriented
towards the
needs of
the child
as a pupil

**THE WELFARE
CURRICULUM**

X   Y   Z

1. (ACADEMIC) EDUCATION   2. (PASTORAL) WELFARE

ACCOMMODATES AND FACILITATES

STRUCTURES
PROCESSES
PROGRAMMES
MANAGEMENT

school to the good of its pupil, the provision of pastoral care is another. Circle 2 represents this, with, in this case, the good of the individual pupil being conceived of as his or her personal (physical, social and emotional) welfare. The aim is less the educated pupil as the secure and happy child and 'Area B represents those activities whose exclusive aim is the *welfare* of the child, and which is organized on the principle that people matter regardless of their educational pursuits' (Best and Ribbins, p. 13). What is distinctive about Area Y is that it is an aspect of the pastoral and educational work of the school which can be undertaken by common activities. Thus this aspect of the 'pastoral curriculum' is justified both in terms of the contribution which it makes to the education of the pupil *and* by the part it plays in meeting the personal needs of the individual child.

If one aspect of the 'pastoral curriculum' can be justified in terms of the contribution which it makes *both* to the educational and to the personal needs of the pupil, another aspect might require a more limited justification. As I have argued earlier, Pring (1984) suggests a distinction between the notion of a 'tutorial programme' as the most obvious place for group work of a developmental kind designed to facilitate the socialization and personal growth of the individual child, and the rest of the pastoral curriculum (p. 151). In a sense tutorial group work requires a curriculum and certainly some of its leading figures have produced fairly elaborate programmes, but they usually stress that it is the purposes and the approaches to such tutorial work which are crucial rather than its specific content and syllabus. For these reasons I have distinguished an aspect of the pastoral curriculum, Area Z, which I have located solely in that part of the work of the school which is concerned with its pastoral and welfare dimensions.

Were a more complete analysis possible within the constraints of this chapter I would draw out the implications for my analysis of that aspect of the work of the school which is concerned with the need for order and discipline (Circle 3). It would, I think, also be possible to locate and represent a number of the other concepts identified and discussed earlier in this paper such as the notion of the 'academic curriculum' (which, in many ways, may well be a version of Area A) and of 'liberal education'. I shall restrict my remarks to the comment that, in the diagram, the notion of 'liberal education' would not be represented by a specified area, rather it seems to have more to do with the kind of orientation which a school gives to aspects of all its activities.

Finally, in my attempt to distinguish and justify the kinds of purposes and activities which are entailed by notions such as 'education for personal, social and moral development', the 'pastoral curriculum' and the 'tutorial programme' I have left myself without a generic term which can be used to cover all these things. Not much turns on the particular words we chose to use but I suggest that the term 'welfare curriculum' may be as appropriate as any other insofar as it calls attention to both the academic, curricular and educational dimension of such work and to its pastoral, personal and welfare aspects.

I have said very little in this discussion about how schools might go about institutionalizing such a welfare curriculum or some particular aspect of it through the development of appropriate structures, processes, programmes and the like. Certainly many writers have tackled these issues (Bulman, 1984; Healy, 1984; Marland, 1980; Mclaughlin, 1982) as we have ourselves in a paper entitled 'Careers Education and the Welfare Curriculum' (Best, *et al.*, 1984). Nor have I attempted to consider the problems of implementation which are likely to be encountered by any teacher or school seeking to innovate in this area. There is a simple explanation for this. Although there is a good deal of evidence that many schools have attempted to innovate in this area, there is, as yet, very little, systematic research on the topic which has been published (see Ribbins and Best, 1985). To that end the Spring 1985 edition of the journal *Pastoral Care in Education* is largely devoted to this theme and contains a number of reports of small scale research dealing with this kind of issue.

Conclusion

In this chapter I have focused on an aspect of schooling that has been the subject of a good deal of innovation within, in particular, the secondary sector. Writing a decade ago about the development of 'pastoral care' we argued that, as with many other educational innovations in this country it was introduced largely as a result of an act of faith rather than as the result of systematic and thorough empirical research as to the educational and social benefits that might be expected. That, furthermore, the debates surrounding such innovations were all too often confused by a lack of clear and shared usage and interpretation of the key concepts involved. That, finally, the actual functioning and consequences of these innovations were frequently not what their advocates had anticipated and were all too often as likely to defeat stated purpose as to achieve them (Best *et al.*, 1977).

Whilst the gap between the growing concern for education for social, personal, moral and emotional development within schools and the subsequent development of a developed corpus of writings on this theme has been much briefer than was the case with 'pastoral care' (see Lang and Ribbins, 1985), it does, nevertheless, seem to have existed. More recently there have been strenuous attempts to 'catch up' and in this chapter I have tried to make a contribution to that part of the literature which has as its purpose the clarification of the key terms and concepts involved and in doing so have felt the need, at some risk of contributing to such confusion as exists, to advocate the need for yet another term — 'The Welfare Curriculum' — to add to the many which already exist. Having made my attempt at conceptual clarification, I am going to try to pull up the drawbridge behind me and suggest that what we really need now is a shift in emphasis. A shift in which less interest is devoted to further attempts at conceptual clarification, or even to the dissemination of advice as to how the institutionalization of a welfare curriculum or some aspect of it ought to be implemented and managed, and much more attention is given to empirical investigations and reports of what is actually happening within schools and colleges.

Control and Welfare: Towards a Theory of Constructive Discipline in Schools

Delwyn Tattum
South Glamorgan Institute of Higher Education

Control and Welfare: Some of the Issues

Where socially undesirable conditions exist or where certain human needs are left unmet, then people experience deprivation and frustration and it is the responsibility of a caring society to seek to alleviate such problems. In Britain we have a welfare state, of which the education system is a part. Within that system teachers are professionally, morally and legally responsible for the welfare of the children in their charge, which means, in broad terms, that they are responsible for their personal and social development. Teachers also stand in *loco parentis* while the child is in school. In recent years the welfare role of teachers has expanded their concern and care into realms beyond the immediate teaching task and into a direct pastoral role, which ideally involves acting as an intermediary between the child and the organization and a link between the school and the family. Furthermore, teachers are responsible for initiating action in making provision for children who are seen to be in special need. This may mean the provision of free meals or clothing grants, visits to the schools' medical services, or even the identification of children with special educational needs. In other words, teachers' social concerns extend into the physical and medical as well as the educational and social needs of a child.

The pursuit of social order has prompted societies to establish places to which persons who display or practise serious deviant forms of behaviour may be transferred. In education we are preoccupied with the *normal* child in the *ordinary* school; but both terms presuppose abnormality and difference. We adopt a soft approach to the segregation of children into special schools as we argue that this enables expertise and resources to be concentrated for the benefit of the handicapped child. However, it might also be true that defective and troublesome pupils create extra demands on the school organization and pose problems for teachers, and therefore their transfer to special schools eases pressures on the teacher and facilitates the smoother running of the 'normal' education sector. Concentration on the social pathology of the individual permits us to ignore deficiencies in the system.

For expressed humanitarian reasons and using the rhetoric of help and needs, care and concern, the categories of pupils deemed as being in need of special education has increased, and the numbers in each category has expanded over recent decades (Tomlinson 1982). In the last decade or so, our identification of a new category of pupil who exhibits social and conduct disorders is consistent with our general pre-occupation to sift out more and more children who do not fit into the model of the normal child in the ordinary school. In fact, the disrupters are particularly apposite to the control-welfare debate, as they, in an overt and dramatic way, challenge the school's authority structure. By definition their behaviour *is* the problem of social control. They disrupt the legitimate activities of school and classroom, and interrupt the learning opportunities of other pupils as well as their own. There are various definitions of a 'disruptive pupil', but for the development of this paper the following is offered. 'It is rule-breaking behaviour in the form of conscious action or inaction, which brings about an interruption or curtailment of a classroom or school activity, and damages personal relationships' (Tattum 1982, p. 46). This definition highlights the importance of rules as a control factor, and it places the act in a context and within a social relationship — factors that are important to the adoption of a constructive approach to discipline.

The speed of the growth of separate provision for disruptive pupils has been as dramatic as that for other special education categories. The peak year for the setting up of units was 1974, but the DES did not act to establish the number and nature of this new kind of provision until summer 1977. They found that sixty-nine of the ninety-six English LEAs had one or more units, giving a total of 239 units providing places for 3962 pupils (HMI 1978). The ACE Survey (1980) confirmed that units existed throughout the United Kingdom, to include Scotland, Wales, the Isle of Man, and the Channel Islands. More recently the Social Education Research Project confirmed that over a five year period from the Inspectorate's survey of 1978 there had been an increase of 140 per cent in off-site units (Ling 1984).

The establishment of units for disruptive pupils further exemplifies the relationship between control and welfare in education as we seek to answer the following three questions:

1   Who Benefits from the Transfer?

There are several groups who may be said to benefit from a pupil's transfer to a unit — the pupil, other pupils, the teacher(s), and the school in general; and yet the disruptive transferee is probably not foremost in people's minds, rather their concern is more likely to be for the other groups. This means that contrary to general practice in Special Education and its implicit philosophy of education, the transfer of a pupil to a unit may be primarily for the welfare of those who do not attend it.

2   Who Decides and on the Basis of What Information?

Local education authorities vary considerably in their admissions procedures and can range from a multi-professional panel with its expert knowledge and information, to a single person — a headteacher, educational psychologist, or an adminstrative officer (Tattum 1982). Furthermore, the procedures employed for gathering information and its presentation are fraught with inadequacies and inconsistencies. Behavioural criteria are problematic and the measurement schedules available, such as the Rutter Scale and the Bristol Social Adjustment Guide, have many limitations. They only describe behaviour and in so doing concentrate on negative aspects; they are filled in by the offended party and must therefore be highly subjective; they focus on the child and fail to take into account teacher-pupil relationships.

3   What are the Functions of Units?

Special units have been referred to as 'sin-bins' and 'mini-borstals', which may not be surprising considering their clients, but it is deeply disturbing if it means that punitive establishments exist within the education service. The function of units has been variously described as *punitive* and *containment* — purposes which are negative and difficult to justify: *diagnostic* and *therapeutic* — which are more positive and yet, in social control terms, are directed towards resocialization. Thirdly, units must have an *educative* function, but for many reasons, not least the inadequacy of buildings and resources, the quality of education available in many is unacceptable (HMI 1978).

The relationship between welfare and control is particularly evident in the specialist function of pastoral care staff. They reflect how schools have more consciously than ever before acknowledged their social function as being, outside the family, the chief means whereby society meets its paramount need to ensure the socialization, well-being, and growth into maturity of its young members. Unfortunately, through their 'rhetoric of caring' (Tattum 1984a), many schools have stimulated expectations in their pupils which they are unable or unwilling to fulfil, and disruptive pupils in particular have highlighted the inconsistencies which exist in a system which professes concern but concentrates on control.

This can be seen starkly in the dual functions pastoral middle managers are expected to undertake which can create severe role-conflict as they try to resolve their disciplinary and punitive duties with their counselling and guidance responsibilities. They spend so much time and energy dealing with the indisciplined minority that there is a real sense in which they neglect the needs of the majority of diligent and well-behaved pupils (Johnson *et al.* 1980).

Furthermore, the academic impetus of schools has an in-built potential for rejecting and hence alienating a significant number of pupils. Therefore, in order to protect the battered self-images of the system's rejects a more constructive approach to discipline is needed, so that all teachers develop counselling skills and cultivate a broader school and curriculum perspective. Teachers are alert to the pressures that families create for pupils, but schools and classrooms too are problem-creating environments. Caring is a professional concern. To care about what happens to your client is integral to the traditional model of the professional person. It means more than the application of specialist knowledge, but also accepting responsibility for the outcomes of one's own initiatives. It is in this way that discipline and welfare are integral to the learning process, and to the creation of a social environment conducive to the personal and social development of its young people.

Towards a More Constructive Approach to Discipline

Too much of our thinking about discipline has started from the wrong end, that is with questions as to how young offenders might be identified, punished and contained rather than how to create learning environments that might encourage productive pupil behaviour. Too often discipline is considered only in the negative context of punishment and criticism, whilst a more positive approach would emphasize the value of praise and encouragement, incentives and inducements. We aim to deal with the disturbances pupils create more in terms of how to control the child and less in terms of·support and help. Children react well to praise; and in a recent document the NAHT (1984) examines 'the positive side of discipline', and gives a comprehensive list of ways schools can use praise and rewards — ranging from a quiet word or public acknowledgement through to 'a letter to parents informing them specifically of some action or achievement deserving praise. (Too often schools write only when something is wrong)' (p. 3). Furthermore, a positive approach needs an even wider consideration of the school as an institution, and the classroom as a microcosm of school life. The character and ethos of a school is determined by, amongst other things, decisions about the curriculum, the allocation of resources, the grouping of pupils, and the arrangements made for guidance and welfare. The social environment of learning is also about the quality of relationships experienced in the intensity of teacher-pupil interaction.

In the first part of this paper I intimated that a misconception exists in schools, which views the experts outside the classroom as having the answers, rather than a more constructive belief in the teacher's own ability to cope with cases of indiscipline. The result is that teachers' confidence in their own capabilities is undermined, and also that the school is not challenged to examine wider issues of internal policies and practices. The points discussed in the section have relevance for teachers in both primary and secondary schools. Recent research indicates that disruptive behaviour is displayed by very young children (Chazan 1983); also that many who work in nursery and infant schools hold too low expectations of the intellectual maturity of children and fail to stimulate their imagination and curiosity (Tizard and Hughes 1984).

A *crisis-management approach* predominates in many schools, waiting for problems to reveal themselves in personal crises or confrontational outbursts. This also emphasises an approach to social control, which is school orientated and geared mainly to deal with the indisciplined minority. By contrast a *problem-prevention approach* is person orientated, in the sense that its concern is for the welfare of all pupils. It entails an approach which is both school-wide and anticipatory and designed to support systematically all children in their personal and social development. It recognizes that tension and conflict are an inevitable aspect of teacher-pupil interaction, but also that the negative aspects of such interactions can be reduced by good classroom management and by the establishment of appropriate interpersonal relations. The two models are shown below in table form; and the rest of this paper will be devoted to the five elements indentified as problem-prevention approach.

Table 1. Two Models of Approach to Discipline in Schools

Crisis-Management Approach	Problem-Prevention Approach
1 Use of official punishments and sanctions — including special units.	1 Development of school and classroom rules.
2 Use of a school's specialist staff — senior pastoral staff, counsellors.	2 Employing effective teaching techniques and skills.
3 Involvement of external agencies — including special education.	3 Developing positive pupils' self-concepts.
4 Negative involvement of parents.	4 Establishing good teacher-pupil relations.
	5 Teaching of personal and social education.

Whilst conscious that the five aspects of a problem-prevention approach to discipline are not independent but overlap each other, the aim is to focus on features of teacher-pupil interaction which bear on the total learning environment and the messages they convey about the school as a caring community.

1 The Development of Appropriate School and Classroom Rules

In research with disruptive pupils I identified five vocabularies of motives (Tattum 1982), as the youngsters explained and justified their behaviour in terms of the school's culture, and they tried to give meaning to their learning and behavioural experiences in their day-to-day contacts with teachers and other pupils. The five categories are:

1 It was the teacher's fault.
2 Being treated with disrespect.
3 Inconsistency of rule application.
4 We were only messing — having a laugh.
5 It's the fault of the school system.

The vocabularies of motives range from blaming teacher to blaming the system, but it is not the general attribution of blame that is important but the specific things that they point to that is of value. For whilst these pupils were the extreme exponents of disruptive behaviour they do not stand in isolation from *all* other pupils, but rather at the negative pole on a continuum of indiscipline. Much of what is developed in the following sections arises directly from what they had to say and from my many visits to special units.

The centrality of rules in the above accounts of disruptive pupils is not surprising, and by the same token one would not advocate that teachers deviate from the known practice of applying the rule to the child and not the offence. The problem though, in a large secondary school, is that is is not possible for a teacher to know every pupil, and so the system presents opportunities for injustices and inequalities. When this happens children are frustrated and disgruntled. In fact, a dilemma that teachers face is maintaining good relationships as they vary between domination and coercion and creating a friendly and cooperative atmosphere in their classroom, (see, for example, Mrs. Chalmers in Best *et al.* 1983, p. 144). No doubt this is one of the reasons why they are less committed to enforcement of 'around school rules' than they are about classroom conduct (Hargreaves *et al.* 1975).

Surprisingly, whilst schools can be described as rule-governed, there has been very little research into rules. In an attempt to more clearly understand the extent and complexity of school rules the following five-fold categorization was drawn up (Tattum 1982).

(a) *Legal/quasi-legal rules* apply to areas such as attendance, punctuality, corporal punishment, suspensions, and appearance. Appearance and style are important to young people, and many resent a teacher's intrusion into what they regard as personal. But rules are expressions of values and attitudes, and more than neatness, decorum and style are involved for both parties.

(b) *Organizational rules* are the general rules necessary for a school's smooth-running and good order. They control the movement of large numbers at set times, identify forbidden places and behaviour, and cover such matters as litter, graffiti etc. Registration, homework, morning assembly and dining room behaviour are regulated, so that rules, ritual and routine pervade school life. But as they move about the school pupils witness and experience differential treatment which makes them aggrieved and disgrunted.

(c) *Contextual rules* pinpoint the variation experienced by pupils as they move from lesson to lesson as different demands are made covering conduct, task and dress. Different rules appertain to the gymnasium, the laboratory, practical rooms and so on; as in each case the physical setting allied to the nature of the subject determines situational constraints and prohibitions. Hargreaves *et al.* (1975) identified and elaborated the situational rules around five themes — talk, movement, time, teacher-pupil and pupil-pupil relationships. Each theme contains a great number of rules, some common to most teachers, such as not talking when teacher is talking — whilst others are more individualistic, such as shouting out an answer or working with a neighbour. Some subjects have more contextual rules than others so that the opportunities for rule-breaking are greater; and also, as different teachers have different priorities and tolerance levels, what constitutes 'deviance' can vary according to each teacher's expectations.

(d) *Personal rules* provide the greatest 'between-teacher' variance. Pupils are an integral part of classroom interaction, and how they perceive the situation will influence the nature of the ensuing negotiations. Part of such negotiation is 'teacher-testing' as each party tests out the other, the purpose of which is to facilitate present and subsequent encounters. 'First encounters' are a time in any interaction when a great deal of interpretive work goes on, and as the classroom initiative usually rests with teachers it is for them to make explicit the parameters of acceptable behaviour. Assuming pupil knowledge about legal, organisation and contextual rules, it is around the personal and relational rules that most negotiation takes place as each individual teacher faces a partially defined situation which needs to be given substance by the teacher's own *modus operandi*. For the pupils it is an accumulative and comparative exercise, and the knowledge they seek is how strictly a teacher

applies contextual rules, and what are that teacher's personal rules (Werthamn 1963).

(e) *Relational rules* reflect the highly personal nature of social
control in schools. The tone of teacher-pupil interaction is
dictated by the teachers. All teachers have to decide on the
social distance they will preserve between themselves and
the pupils, and experienced teachers advise new entrants to
keep initial contacts formal and only gradually narrow the
deference gap. Because of the size of secondary schools a
great deal of teacher-pupil contact is at the formal or
semi-formal level, which is another reason why pupils are
differentially treated. Teachers look for clues of a personal
nature as they question pupils, assessing appearance and
demeanour. Some pupils are more adept at giving acceptable explanations of their behaviour, and at adopting the
appropriate posture and tone when challenged. Lufler
(1979) found evidence that students from lower socio-
economic backgrounds were disproportionately sent to the
principal's office, and interview data indicated that 'some
teachers saw lower-class children as potentially more disruptive and therefore as requiring more punishment'.

Discipline is a personal matter and it is the area in which teachers
are made to feel individually accountable by colleagues. Teaching is
also a public activity and so teachers lay great store on 'keeping face'.
It is this sense of vulnerability which may explain why the profession
devotes so much more time to criticizing bad behaviour than to
rewarding good behaviour.

Social control in schools is a complex problem, of which the rule
system is only a part; and the ways schools organise themselves
influences relationships and the levels of pupil disaffection. As
person-changing organizations schools need to examine their person-
management methods, and the following recommendations are made
regarding rules:

(i) First, both teachers and pupils should become more closely involved in the creation and review of rules. More
open-discussion will bring better understanding of control
methods and their related problems. Teachers work in the
isolation of their classroom for much of the time; and
rarely does a school give time for teachers and pupils to
discuss the rationale and justification of its rule system
(HMI 1982).

(ii) Second, rules must be communicated to teachers, pupils and parents. Social control is based on the supposition that knowledge of the rules exists among members, and so they must be articulated if uncertainty and inconsistencies are to be reduced.

(iii) Third, it is important to have as few rules as possible.

(iv) Fourth, teachers should set themselves as models in their own dress and behaviour, in the way they talk to and treat young people, and by arriving for lessons on time and well-prepared.

It is evident that these recommendations also apply to classrooms, for they relate to the principles that teachers should introduce their pupils to the democratic processes, and that individuals support and implement decisions they have helped to make.

2   *Employing Effective Teaching Techniques and Skills*

We need to dispense with the commonly held view that teachers are born and not made. People who talk in this vein refer to personality and charisma; and whilst not dismissing the significance of individual characteristics we have to beware of reducing the craft of teaching to intuition. Teaching is a highly skilled activity which should and can be improved through study, experiment and practice.

The importance of effective teaching in preventing unproductive pupil behaviour may be illustrated by Kounin's (1970) research into classroom discipline. He found that the differences between effective teachers and those who had major management problems lay essentially in the successful teacher's ability to prevent discipline problems from arising. Kounin (1970) advises that we attend to what occurs just prior to misbehaviour rather than immediately afterwards. The positive approach is to improve the conditions that gave rise to unwanted behaviour rather than stressing consequences and punishments. The latter may have short-term results but does not address fundamental questions concerning the appropriateness of the teaching, the relevance of the curriculum, or the quality of the relationships (see also Brophy and Everston 1975).

Successful teachers were found to be better prepared and organized, and moved smoothly from one activity to another. They also maintained pupil involvement in activities by clear instructions and guidance, and not interrupting class instructions to follow other issues. Kounin also noted that the more effective teachers had greater class awareness, as they scanned for potential problems and so dealt with them before they became real difficulties. They also anticipated pupils' needs and minimized restlessness and boredom through work that was interesting and matched the pupils' abilities. Hargreaves *et al.* (1975) examined 'switch-signalling', aimed to cue pupils at the starting or ending of an activity. Secondary teachers who gave clear, unambiguous signals were discovered to have fewer problems than those who gave none or who were imprecise. Other features of good class control highlighted in recent research are the pacing of lessons, the importance of eye contact, and the significance of personal space for teachers and pupils.

Concern about low teacher expectations has regularly been expressed in published HM Inspectors' reports. In *Inviting School Success* Purkey and Novak (1984), define the teacher as an inviter who sends out messages through formal and informal, verbal and non-verbal, conscious and unconscious ways to inform students that they are 'valuable, able and responsible, that they have opportunities to participate meaningfully in worthwhile activities, and that they are invited to take advantage of these opportunities'. Conversely, a disinviting message informs people that they are irresponsible, incapable and worthless.

Perhaps the best-known study of the expectancy factor in teaching is that of Rosenthal and Jacobson (1968), who reported success in influencing pupil performance by giving teachers favourable data about selected pupils. And whilst the methodology of this work has been criticized its critics have not questioned the basic assumption that teachers' attitudes influence pupil self perception, behaviour and performance.

In brief, teachers tend to exhibit more positive non-verbal behaviour to pupils considered bright than to those considered dull. These behaviours are expressed in tone of voice, body stance, facial expressions, gestures and physical proximity. Teachers also teach more to, spend more time with, and request more from pupils they consider able (Baker and Crist 1971). Less able pupils are given fewer opportunities to respond, are given less time to answer, and are substantially more likely to be criticized for incorrect responses than their high-achieving classmates. As Brophy and Good (1974) concluded from their extensive research on the communication of expectation, many youngsters are given an impoverished learning experience. Finally, Burns (1982) offers four recommendations on how teachers may counter the negative aspects of the expectancy effect: (i) interact evenly with all pupils; (ii) talk with all pupils; (iii) praise pupils realistically; and (iv) set tasks to suit individuals.

3 Developing Positive Pupils' Self-concepts

The links between this section and the previous one are obvious. From my own research with disruptive pupils it was evident that they often held negative views of themselves as learners; as one boy said, 'School is for learning, but all it learnt me is that I'm no good for anything' (Tattum 1982, p. 179). A measure of success and achievement is important, otherwise why attend school or pay attention to lessons. Research by Branch *et al.* (1977) reveals a significant relationship between low self-concept as a learner and misbehaviour in the classroom. They evaluated disruptive and non-disruptive middle-school students (eleven to fourteen years) on their professed and inferred academic self-concepts. Those students identified by their behaviour as disruptive had significantly lower self-concepts as learners than did students identified as non-disruptive. The theoretical implication drawn from the study was that students' negative feelings about themselves as learners may be a contributory factor in student disruption, and that self-concept may eventually prove to be a significant mediating variable that will help us understand many types of seemingly unrelated behaviour problems.

In their report on 'Improving secondary schools' in the ILEA, the Committee identified four achievement aspects (Hargreaves 1984): the capacity to memorize and organise knowledge; the ability to apply knowledge to problem-solving situations; the capacity to communicate and cooperate with others; and the fourth, motivation and commitment, is regarded as a prerequisite of the previous three. Lack of motivation is seen to originate in social class background, and some schools may actively reduce motivation and commitment in pupils thereby causing further underachievement in aspects one to three:

> If the school does not attend to aspect IV as a central feature of its work, then achievement in the other three aspects becomes improbable. When the school believes it is not within its powers to influence aspect IV, the teachers begin to explain the lack of achievement in terms of the pupils' background, and these low teacher expectations become self-fulfilling. And when pupils experience their schooling as

a threat to their aspect IV achievement, it becomes rational for them to play truant or to protect themselves by classroom misbehaviour.

Two observations might be made on all this. Firstly, despite the evidence supporting the advantages of enhancing pupils' self-concepts many teachers argue that their role is to teach subject matter and not to change personalities, ignoring the fact that they work in a person-changing institution. Secondly, and the Report surprisingly fails to make this point, labelling youngsters as unmotivated, ignores the underlying problem of a negative self-concept. People high in their own estimation approach tasks and other people with the expectation that they will be successful and well-received. Many of the pupils interviewed (Tattum 1984b) regarded themselves as 'system rejects', as they believed that teachers were not interested in them as persons or pupils, and their response was apathy, withdrawal, or open defiance.

A practice that contributes to the development of a negative self-concept is that of labelling, and the negative consequences of labelling may outweigh the intended benefits of attempts to meet the needs of pupils who require special help.

> Categories and labels are powerful instruments for social regulation and control, and they often are employed for obscure, covert or hurtful purposes; to degrade people, to deny them access to opportunity, to exclude 'undesirables' whose presence in society in some way offends, disturbs familiar customs, or demands extraordinary efforts (Hobbs 1975).

Beyond the formal school policies of suspending, ascertainment and transfer, streaming and banding, many pupils complain of being 'treated with disrespect' (Tattum 1982), as either intentionally or unintentionally, teachers cause them to experience embarrassment, frustration and failure.

> 'Talk to us like a dog. Telling you straight now, they're terrible, can't talk to you nice. And that's what makes me go mad then see. If someone shouts at me I got to shout back at them. If a teacher hits me I got to hit them back,' said thirteen year old Debbie.

Here she expresses one way whereby some youngsters seek to protect their self-images, as they return the verbal, physical and organization assaults on their perceptions of self with similar abuse. To be passive is a denial of self and a loss of self-respect. Garfinkel (1956) calls such public demeaning acts 'degradation ceremonies', as they devalue the self through subjection to embarrassment, confusion and humiliation.

In the light of the findings related so far on the relationship between effective teaching strategies, pupils' self-concepts, and behaviour, it is important to note findings that indicate that many youngsters view school as a discouraging and undesirable place to be. If we are therefore to approach problem behaviour more positively we must create learning environments that meet pupils' personal and academic needs. Even the most disruptive of pupils do not behave so with all their teachers, particularly those they perceive as genuinely caring and interested in their work and progress.

4 *Establishing Good Teacher-Pupil Relations*

The school as a caring community only has meaning through the quality of the relationships that exist; and if positive approaches to discipline are to be effective then much depends on how well teachers and pupils relate to each other. Children need to feel that they belong and that adults care about them, and this is as true of school life as it is true of family life. Pupils can be highly critical of teachers who they perceive as being unconcerned or uninterested in them. 'Some teachers don't want to know and don't care', was the comment of one disruptive girl. Caring personalizes the relationship, and for the pupil it is an opportunity to get behind the formal teacher role into an association that has meaning — the human side of schooling. Wilson (1962) emphasized the importance of affective bonds in a society in which most role relationships are neutral.

The instrumental and affective aspects of teaching are interwoven and both are essential ingredients of an effective learning environment. The therapeutic value inherent in providing individuals with a sense of being cared for and respected is at the heart of the work of Carl Rogers. In describing the ingredients of a relationship which facilitates positive personal growth and learning, he writes,

> There is another attitude which stands out in those who are successful in facilitating learning ... I think of it as prizing the learner, prizing his feelings, his opinions, his person. It is a caring for the learner, but a non-possessive caring. It is an acceptance of this other individual as a separate person, having worth in his own right (Rogers 1969).

Research into the 'good teacher' also confirms the importance of both the instrumental and affective areas. Grace (1978) asked head teachers to designate which members of their staff they regarded as 'outstanding' teachers within the context of the inner-city comprehensive school. Poor teachers were seen to be lazy, weak and ineffectual in their classroom organization, and lacked commitment to the welfare of their pupils. By comparison, good teachers were characterized by hard work, a good rapport with pupils, 'and a demonstration of an individualistic welfare commitment to the various distresses of inner-city pupils'. Supportive findings come from the work of Metz (1978), who looked at the ways different teachers legitimized their authority in four junior schools. With the most difficult pupils successful teachers imposed a clear structure on classroom activities, gave the impression of confidence and competence in their teaching, and finally, they treated the students with regard and respect even when they reproached or disciplined them.

Turning to the views of the pupils, Weston *et al.* (1978), in a survey of the attitudes towards schooling of thirteen and fourteen year olds, found that regardless of social background or ability, pupils regarded it as a teacher's function to assist them in their personal and social development, and create a happy and supportive ethos within the school. Wood (1978) makes the telling point from his extended conversations with over two hundred fourth and fifth year pupils that for many the intrinsic value of work was alien to their thinking; they were much more interested in the kind of relationships the work situation offered with friends and teachers. If the relationships were tolerable then the work was much less burdensome; in fact, a friendly teacher could make school work pleasant and enjoyable. Wood concludes that 'the simple moral is to make work count, and for teachers to be human'.

Sadly, research by Thompson (1975) into what pupils find particulary lacking in teachers, revealed that these are the very qualities which make them human. In comparison with other adults pupils rated teachers more favourably on their primary role qualities such as interesting, wise, successful — but hard. On qualities such as kindness, fairness and warmth they were less favourably rated. Disruptive pupils openly admitted that their behaviour in the classroom was determined by their attitude towards the teacher, whether he showed kindness and understanding, and was friendly and helpful. It is suggested that a predominantly utilitarian approach to the teacher's role, focusing on instructional and disciplinary functions, fails to take into account the expectations of pupils and can result in the hostile attitudes found by Corrigan (1979). In response to a statement, 'Teachers don't really care about what happens to me they are just doing a job', of the ninety-three teenage boys involved in his study, sixty-two agreed or strongly agreed with the statement.

The value placed on peer group relationships is well documented, and disruptive pupils explained much of their misbehaviour as 'only messing about — having a laugh' with friends (Tattum 1982). In a recent study into the social life of classrooms in an Australian high school, Macpherson (1983) looks at classroom interaction, the peer group as a socializing agent, and how students construct their positions of dominance and determine the use of classroom norms. He is critical of teachers' ignorance of the social life that exists in any classroom, and their lack of commitment to this aspect of interpersonal relations. He concludes that teachers 'are too concerned with their subject matter and their order to know students' values and social structure'.

5   *Teaching of Personal and Social Education*

Whilst this section overlaps with the previous one on relationships it is different in that it takes us into the area of the curriculum. Explicit in the last section was the belief that responsibility for good relations is part of teaching, and should not be left to the efforts of a few committed individuals with pastoral responsibilities. Caring for and teaching the child are so much bound together as to be inseparable. But I want to stress the responsibility that school's have for developing a programme for the personal and social education for all of its pupils, a point developed at some length by Ribbins in an earlier chapter.

At this point I will only reiterate the view expressed in a recent ILEA report on *Improving Secondary Schools* that:

> social and personal education at its best is an important bridge between the pastoral and academic aspects of the school's work and should serve to integrate a wide range of the school's aims and practices (Hargreaves 1984).

Conclusion

These tentative steps towards a more constructive approach to discipline have concentrated on seeking ways whereby we can create a secure and healthy environment that is conductive to the personal and social development of children. The emphasis has been on teacher initiated behaviour; it involves planning prior to the school year, each day and each lesson. In many respects it requires changes in emphasis to a revision of many entrenched professional attitudes. It also means having regard for youngsters as 'developing centres of consciousness' (Peters 1966), and respecting them as persons and pupils. It is not claimed that the approach will eliminate indiscipline, but rather that concentration on positive, problem-prevention approaches will reduce it, and in so doing take some of the strain and tension out of teacher-pupil interaction to the welfare of both parties.

Schools and a Multi-Professional Approach to Welfare

John Welton
University of London Institute of Education

The traditional restricted professionalism of school teachers and their advisers limits their effectiveness in meeting children's needs. Despite the development of pastoral care curricula, tutorial and counselling systems, and the greater attention paid in recent years to home-school relations, the traditional concept of the school has not changed:

> Schools are concerned with the educational development of children. The proper job of the teacher is to teach. It is dangerous for teachers to get involved in meeting the social and other needs of children and in any case they do not have time. The sole purpose of pastoral care and the promotion of good home-school relations is to enable childern to have access to education.

Where such teachers have explicit views of the social purpose of schools they tend to echo the cultural missionary component of the compensatory education era in the 1950s and 1960s. Education is seen as a means to social mobility, economic and moral salvation. Teaching as social reproduction, that is, enabling children to become like the teacher!

However more enlightened teachers know that their work does not stand apart from that of other professionals and services working for children and families. If children's needs, including those for education, are to be met most effectively our concept of the school has to change. Teacher roles and training have to change. The strength of coupling between education and other welfare sectors has to change. The pastoral care lobby in education will have to refocus from the myopia of assuming that welfare systems in schools merely serve the pedagogic system, to a stereoscopic, three dimensional vision of the teachers' role in:-

1   meeting the educational need of children,
2   screening for childrens' other welfare needs,
3   referring children to, and cooperating with other welfare agencies.

The idea that schools are an integral part of the welfare network for children and young people is not easily accepted either by teachers, or other professionals working with children and their families. Schools, like the other welfare services have grown up in their own professional and administrative enclave, developing incrementally in response to a growing awareness of need which triggered an administrative and political threshold for the release of resources. Each welfare sector, be it medical, personal social services, employment, housing, social security or education, developed its own political, professional and administrative framework. Separate departments were formed for policy making and administration at central and local government levels. Professional training developed for the most part in specialist departments and institutes, which socialize their novices into the tunnel vision of their own profession. Research and development work in service delivery tends to be carried out in specialist research units associated with professional training, and disseminated via professional journals which are rarely read by members of other professions working with the same clients. How many health and social service professionals and adminstrators will read this book published in the 'Contemporary Analysis in Education Series', although its theme is closely related to their work? Will the publishers even think of advertizing it in the health and social service press? The development of multi-professional work is itself inhibited by the social division of dissemination!

The twentieth century expansion of services concerned with meeting the needs of children has led to a social division of welfare which has both functional and disfunctional aspects. Fundamental to the concept of professional welfare work is the special and confidential relationship between the client and professional helper. However the needs of clients rarely lie entirely within the competence of a single profession. Further, although each welfare specialism developed to meet particular client needs, circumstances change, and as knowledge grows about the causes and possible responses to need, so the original core of professional knowledge, services and tasks extends. Compared with even ten years ago the medical profession contains a vast range of specialist occupational roles. Similarly, the title *teacher* summarizes a variety of pedagogic, administrative and therapist roles. Despite the integrative concept of *generic social worker* promoted in the Seebohm Report (1968), specialist roles are reappearing within social work teams.

While the various needs of children and families may be provided for by separate legislation, administrative structures and professional services, they are not experienced separately by the family, the child/patient/client as variously described. Twenty years ago, as a young research worker I attended a multi-professional team meeting on a west country council estate attended by all the various professionals and administrators concerned with meeting the needs of local families. At each fortnightly meeting the medical, educational, social work, housing and other staff compared notes on the progress of work with various families. These meetings enabled a rational planning of work to avoid overlap of intervention. A key member of the team was the Education Welfare Worker. Schools are a universal service to which children relate as a matter of course — a normal relationship, without the danger of stigma rather than one which stems from some social or medical pathology. During these meetings the potential which schools have for screening for social and medical as well as educational need was demonstrated. When a family experienced difficulties it almost invariably became apparent in the behaviour of children in school. Most of the families discussed at the fortnightly team meetings were known to the Educational Welfare Officer, whose close links with the local school teachers enabled him to carry out a screening role for potential problems.

The welfare network exists at the level of both normal and crisis care. Families, schools and communities provide normal support but where this is insufficient or absent, specialist help may be brought in to action. Specialist support reinforces normal support within the home, community or school environment, and in extreme cases removes a child or adult to provide protection or give access to the social, medical or educational resources needed. As they grow older children experience a gradually widening contact with individuals and organizations concerned with their care and development. The family is supplemented by a wider framework of friends and neighbours. Specialist intervention starts with the medical doctor, midwife and health visitor; later, playleaders and teachers induct children into wider institutional and community roles.

While it can be argued that schools are not designed, and teachers not trained to treat social or medical problems, they provide a unique opportunity for screening almost the total population of children and young people during critical periods of their development. It is now taken for granted that schools should be used for medical screening. The school meals service was established partly to ensure minimum standards of nutrition although this policy has been eroded in recent years. Less universally or explicitly accepted has been the opportunity which schools provide to screen for the general welfare and security of children. The alert, concerned and well trained classroom teacher backed up by experienced senior colleagues and in some cases by counsellors, can identify children who are at risk in various ways and draw them to the attention of the appropriate profession or agency.

Professional Response to the Various Needs of Children

Part of the fear which teachers and other professionals have of accepting a broad conception of their professional role may arise from failure to distinguish clearly between different forms of response to need. During the early stages of a recent research project, Welton and Henderson (1980) found considerable differences within as well as between professions in the breadth of their role conception. During interviews some professionals had a very clear idea of the limits of their professional responsibilities, others were less clear. Welton and Henderson concluded that:

1　The various professions and services working with children and families were at different stages in their professional development.
2　While each profession had a different role to play there was some overlap both between their concerns and the tasks which they perform.
3　Within each profession individuals differed in the breadth of their role conception. Some respondents took a restricted view of their work, focusing on the traditional core, for example the pedagogic role of the teachers or the clinical medical role of the doctor. Other respondents took a more extended view, relating their core concerns to other client needs, while recognizing the need to integrate their work with that of others within their own or another profession working with the same child or family.
4　Professionals differed in the way in which they responded to

the need to exchange confidential information with other professions.

5 Many professionals failed to distinguish different types of professional response to need:

    a *Treatment* — a direct professional response to meet a child's need for education, health, security etc. which is part of the core competence of a profession.

    b *Referral* — a professional response of referring a child or family to the appropriate source of *Treatment* either to a specialist within the same profession, or to another profession. This is a key screening role which all profession have, and needs to be formally recognized in their initial and further professional training.

    c *Cooperation* — a professional response of meeting the need of a child or family by working in cooperation with another specialist within the same profession, or in another profession. A mode of working which enables the mobilization of complementary professional skills.

In order to test the extent to which professionals were orientated to a restricted or extended response to the full range of child's needs Welton and Henderson developed a questionnaire on multi-professional work and perspectives, designed to explore issues raised by professionals in an earlier series of pilot interviews. Using a categorization of children's needs adopted from Pringle's *The Needs of Children* (1980) respondents were invited to indicate whether their profession or agency dealt with the child's needs for: material security, maintenance of health and fitness, protection from physical danger, protection from moral danger, social adjustment, emotional and psychological development, cultural and social development, and educational development.

Where they had a professional responsibility to deal with an area of need, they were asked whether they dealt with it entirely by themselves (treatment), or in cooperation with another named profession. Alternatively, respondents could report a professional concern to ensure a child's need was met, but recognizing that their profession did not have the expertise in that area they could indicate to which other profession they would refer the child for help.

Table 1 summarizes the responses of each professional sample to the question about whether and how their profession dealt with the

Table 1. *Professional Orientation to Work with Various needs of Children*

Needs of Children	Social Workers	Probation Officers	Health Visitors	School Nurses	Medical Officers	Educational Psychologist	Educational Welfare Officers	Pastoral Teachers	Academic Teachers
Material security	2% C Hg SB HV	3% R SW Hg HV	0% C SW Hg SB	16% R HV SW SB Hg	11% R SW Hg	54% R SW	4% R SW Hg	36% R SW HV SN V	49% R SW EWO MO N V Hg
Maintenance of health and fitness	26% R GP HV SN MO	23% R SW GP HV	0% C GP H	2% C MO GP H SW	0% C HV SN GP H	17% R MO SW	14% R MO SW	15% C P H EP HV SN GP MO EWO	13% R MO GP SN P EWO Po
Protection from physical danger	2% C GP HV SN MO H Po	7% R SW N Po	0% C SW MO CP N	2% C SW HV GP	4% C SW HV GP	4% R SW MO	0% R N SW	8% C SW HV SN EP N P	10% R EWO SW SN P MO N
Protection from moral danger	1% C Po GP H Pr Sc	0% C SW Po Sc	0% C SW GP Po Sc	16% C SW HV Po	14% C SW HV SN	13% R SW	3% R SW Po N	5% C EWO SW Po V HV SN P MO	16% C Cl Po EWO SW
Social adjustment	3% C Ps CG EP Sc Y	0% C SW EP Sc Y	3% EP Sc GP Ps CG	19% C EP HV MO Ps CG	14% C EP CG Ps	8% C Ps CG	4% R EP SW Sc CG	0% C EP EWC SW	19% C EP P EWO
Emotional and psychological development	2% C Ps CG EP Sc GP	0% C EP Ps CG Sc	0% C EP Sc GP Ps CG	0% C EP HV MO Sc SW	0% C EP CG HV SN MO	4% C Ps CG Ps CG	1% R EP Sc CG	5% C EWO P EP CG	5% C EP P MO

Cultural and social development								
21% C Sc EB V EP	7% C Y EB V Sc	10% C Sc Y V SW	40% R EP Sc V MO	50% R SW	17% C SW Sc V	20% R Sc Y EP	13% S SW Y EWO	15% S P Y EP SW
Educational development								
54% R Sc EP EWO	13% C Sc EB	34% R Sc EP Sp	49% C MO EP Sc	11% C EP Sp Sc	8% C Sc	32% R EP Sc	10% S PT EP	4% S EP P
n = 94	n = 29	n = 61	n = 41	n = 28	n = 24	n = 101	n = 39	n = 402

NEEDS OF CHILDREN

Social Workers

Material Security

2% C Hg SB HV

Key:

percentage who indicate they have *no* professional responsibility to deal with that need

Modal form of reaction to the need:-
S = Dealt with entirely by my own profession or agency
C = Dealt with within my profession *but* — in close co-operation with other agencies
R = Not dealt with by my profession *but* it's part of my professional responsibility to refer to another agency.

Agency with which a profession would cooperate, or make a referral in order that a child's need be met:

CG = Child Guidance Unit
Cl = Clergy
EB = Education and Library Board
EP = Educational Psychologist
EWO = Educational Psychology
GP = General Practitioner
H = Hospital
Hg = Housing Executive
HV = Health Visitor
MO = Medical Officer
N = NSPCC
P = Parent

Po = Police
Pr = Probation Officer
Ps = Psychiatrist
PT = Peripatetic Teacher
SB = Supplementary Benefits
Sc = School
SN = School Nurse
Sp = Speech Therapist
SW = Social Worker
V = Voluntary Organisation
Y = Youth Worker

various needs of children. The teacher sample is divided into those whose work is mainly pastoral in orientaion, and those in mainly academic roles. The percentage indicated at the row/column intersection records the proportion of respondents who indicated that their profession or agency did not deal with that aspect of a child's need. For example, only two per cent of social workers sampled felt that their profession did not deal with aspects of a child's need for material security, whereas over twenty-six per cent felt that they did not deal with matters of health and fitness. Next to the percentage figure in each intersect the letter C, R or S indicates the modal (most frequent) response of those respondents who reported that their profession dealt with an aspect of a child's need. C indicates that the respondents thought that the need would be partly dealt with within their profession but required close cooperation with the work of another profession; they were then asked to specify the other profession. R indicates that the need would not be dealt with directly by members of their profession, but that it is part of their professional responsibility to refer the matter to another (specified) profession, S indicates that the respondents felt that the aspect of need could be met entirely within their own profession. Below the percentage and CRS letters, the professions or agencies named by respondents for cooperation or referral are listed. For example, social workers felt that they could deal with problems of material security in cooperation with housing, supplementary benefits or health visitors, but tended to feel that matters of health and fitness were outside their capabilities for direct action and should be referred to a general practitioner, health visitor, school nurse or school medical officer.

The two most striking findings summarized in Table 1 are, firstly, the very broad professional orientation of the professions sampled, and secondly, the very few cases where respondents claim that a child's needs can be met entirely within their own profession or agency. With certain exceptions it may be concluded that each profession sampled had a broad rather than restricted view of its responsiblity for children's needs, and that in general the respondents recognized the necessity of working in some way with members of other professions either in co-operation or by referring children to them.

Aspects of children's needs about which there was greatest unanimity of professional responsibility were protection from moral danger, and emotional and psychological development, followed by social adjustment and protection from physical danger. Differences were found in their orientation to needs for material security and the maintenance of health and fitness. With the marked exception of the education welfare officers (EWOs) the education service professions (teachers and educational psychologists) were much less clearly orientated to catering for the child's needs for material security than were the medical and welfare professions. even so over half the teachers sampled felt that they had some responsibility for such needs, mainly through referring children to the appropriate profession or agency.

The two areas of children's needs which most clearly highlight differences in professional orientation were cultural and social development and educational development. Only one half of the medical officers and sixty per cent of the school nurses felt that their profession had a responsibility for cultural and social development compared with ninety-three per cent of probation officers, ninety per cent of health visitors and eighty-five per cent of teachers. It is intriguing to wonder about either the linguistic niceties, or more seriously about the professional self concepts of the fifteen per cent of teachers who did not feel they had a responsibility for this area of need! It is in the area of educational development and cultural and social development that most teachers felt that their own profession could cope on its own without referral or cooperation with another profession or agency. However teachers were not alone in feeling responsibility for a child's educational development, for example, nearly ninety per cent of both medical officers and probation officers claimed that they dealt in some way with the educational development of children. Education is not synonymous with schooling.

There is some indication in the data summarized in Table 1 of a negative relationship between a profession's perception of its obligation to work to meet a particular need, and its practice in referring a child to another agency. If a profession is strongly divided about its responsibility for a particular area of need it is unlikely that the matter will form a part of the traditional core of its professional work with children. It should be remembered that professions are not static, and Table 1 may reflect developments which seek to incorporate areas of work into a new and extended professional role which have not yet been fully accepted throughout a profession.

There is not space in this chapter to go into all the indications of professional orientation which are revealed in the survey, but one striking indication concerns the educational welfare service whose dominant reported form of intervention is to refer children to other agencies rather than deal with children's needs directly. This finding appears to reinforce the view of the educational welfare officer as a very important screening and referral agent, who needs the training and experience to recognize a very wide range of need and to whom they may be most appropriately referred. The screening and referral role is very important both within professions (the intake role) and more broadly in the welfare net. Unfortunately, since there are so many different policy, administrative and professional bodies involved, the inter-professional screening and referral role of the educational welfare service does not always get the recognition and credit which it deserves.

The effectiveness of the school as an agency for welfare screening depends firstly on the way in which school-based professionals are prepared for the task of identifying and responding to children's needs. This screening role has implications for both pre-service and in-service training of teachers. Secondly, it requires adequate systems of pastoral care, including methods of record keeping which ensure a continuity of information, good systems of referral and communication within the school, and regular monitoring of the effectiveness of pastoral care as experienced by both children and staff. Thirdly, schools need to establish good channels of communication and cooperation with the various school-attached and community-based welfare organizations which work with the same population.

As I have written elsewhere (Welton 1982, 1983) the various professions and services working with school-age children may be categorized as *School Based* (mainly teachers), *School Attached* or *Community Based*. The school-attached professions such as the educational psychologist, educational welfare officer, or school nurse, work mainly with and through schools, dependent for their work on the relationship which they develop with teachers and school administrators. Community-based professions such as social workers, police juvenile liaison officers, probation officers, and general practitioners have school-age children as only part of their client group and see the school as just one of the several institutions to which their clients may relate. Conflict may arise from differences in the importance which the various professionals attach to different areas of a child's needs. For example, the school-based and school-attached professions may attach greater importance to a child's school attendance than a social worker who views the child in the context of the needs of the family, or a probation officer who in a particular case puts maintaining school attendance at a lower priority than attending to other immediate needs.

While school medical personnel have an identifiable technology, a distinctive range of skills and tasks which establish their position within the school welfare net; educational psychologists and educational welfare officers appear to have greater difficulty in establishing their rationale and relationship with school-based staff. Teachers occupy the central roles in relation to the traditional goals of schools but educational psychologists and educational welfare officers occupy more marginal positions in the school organization, their work is not fully understood by many teachers, or fully integrated into the academic and pastoral care systems. One of the characteristics of the welfare network which inhibits the development of cooperation is the lack of knowledge and understanding which professions have of each other or even of some of the specialisms within their own professions. For example, some teachers are just as confused about the work of their colleagues who take the role of school counsellor, as they are about the work of the social worker or educational psychologist.

Each welfare profession has characteristics (beliefs and attitudes as well as skills and knowledge) which distinguish them from, and maintain their separateness from other professions. In the case of teachers, cooperation with welfare specialists within or outside school may be inhibited by a tendency to reject the experience of colleagues or other professions who do not share the day-to-day experience of classroom life. Medical doctors may hold views about professional preparation and competence which inhibit their cooperation with teachers or social workers, particularly over sharing information. Successful cooperation depends on mutual trust and understanding, based on a recognition of what each specialist activitity can contribute to meet a child's needs.

Rather than knowledge and understanding, the welfare network is riddled with myths and ignorance about the work of other professions, some of which are based on occupational stereotypes, others on ignorance of developments in a particular profession. Common myths include the beliefs that most educational welfare officers are ex-policemen with two left feet; teachers cannot be trusted with confidential information; social workers are young, inexperienced and idealistic do-gooders who are here today and gone tomorrow; medical doctors refuse to share information, and psychologists are usually in need of their own attention! Some beliefs are based on service stereotypes learned in training but not taking account of current practice and characteristics. Others are applied generally as a halo effect following some idiosyncratic critical incident involving a member of that service.

Research (Welton and Henderson 1979) has shown that although negative views may be held about other professions, they may be held by people who have had very little contact with that profession. For example, a positive relationship has been shown to exist between the amount of contact head teachers have, and the degree of satisfaction felt with their working relationships with other services and professions. This relationship was reflected in the findings from a survey of the degree of contact between secondary schools head teachers, and their satisfaction with the working relationship with different services is shown in Table 2. Initial interviews with teachers and members of school-attached and community-based professions working with schoolchildren suggested that even where there was little or infrequent contact with another service, views were held (sometimes very strongly) on their work. Teachers from 191 secondary schools were asked to use a five point scale to indicate how satisfied they were with their working relationship with various professions. A score of five would represent a very satisfactory working relationship and a score of one indicates a very unsatisfactory relationship.

Table 2 shows that the lowest recorded contact was, not suprisingly with the voluntary agency (NSPCC) with the fewest full time workers. The highest mean score on the five point scale of satisfaction is given to the school nurse followed by the educational welfare officer, clergy and police. A trend is shown in the table for

Table 2. *Proportion of Schools in Contact and Satisfaction with Working Relationships Between Secondary School Teachers and Various Professions.*

Profession	Percentage of Teachers in Contact	Mean Score for Satisfaction	Standard Deviation
School Nurse	91	4.5	0.69
Education Welfare Officer	87	4.4	0.27
Clergy	88	4.4	0.8
Police	82	4.4	0.74
Health Visitor	89	4.2	0.77
General Practitioner	72	4.1	1.05
Youth Worker	90	3.9	0.91
Educational Psychologist	89	3.8	1.1
NSPCC Inspector	23	3.8	0.8
Social Worker	72	3.5	1.25
Probation Officer	43	3.4	1.14

Number of teachers (each from a different secondary school) = 191

Correlation between degree of contact and level of satisfaction r = .64

schools to give higher and more uniform scores for satisfaction to services with which they had most contact. This relationship is reflected in the correlation of r = .64 between contact with the service, and the degree of satisfaction expressed in their working relationship with that service.

Youth workers and educational psychologists were shown to be in contact with a high percentage of the schools, but the lower mean scores and greater standard deviation suggests that the teachers are less satisfied with their working relationship with these professions than with the school nurses and educational welfare officers who are also employed by the local education authority. The written comments which the teachers made to accompany their rating for each profession, indicated a desire for more information about, and more contact with social workers, educational psychologists and probation officers. The services to which the teachers gave low scores indicating a less satisfactory working relationship were penalised for lack of accessibility, lower degree of regular contact, and failure to feedback information to schools.

Although Table 2 only indicates the interprofessional working relationship as reported by teachers in 191 schools, a similar relationship was reported between degree of contact, and satisfaction with the working relationship with other professionals by all the other professions surveyed. It can be postulated that in some cases contact between professionals, whether in the same service, or in another service may lead to a greater degree of dissatisfaction. Indeed in the same research, cases were found where a critical incident between members of two professions inhibited further trust and contact between their two services. The more general finding was that the more contact which occurred between professionals, the greater the degree of knowledge, trust, understanding, and willingness to cooperate in meeting the needs of their common client. In the welfare network, absence does not appear to make the heart grow fonder.

Professional confidentiality is an important factor affecting the development of multi-professional cooperation. The exchange of confidential information may in certain cases be essential to the immediate safety of a child particularly in cases of child neglect or abuse. In less critical cases, cooperation may still be important and ways have to be established to allow information and advice to be exchanged between professionals without affecting the crucial relationship of trust between the professional and client (Dick 1983).

Refusal to divulge information may be regarded as good practice within a profession but be misunderstood or resented by another, particularly where members of one profession expect to receive information from another, without expecting to reciprocate by feeding back results. An unwillingness to share information can be interpreted rightly or wrongly, as implying doubt about professional status and competence, leading to a resentment which may inhibit future cooperation. For example, Welton and Dwyer (1982) found that educational welfare officers, conscious of their developing professional status resented a relationship which required them to provide information about children and families for educational psychologists who did not reciprocate with relevant information when the educational welfare officer felt it would be necessary. Another consequence of a refusal to feedback information is to reduce the opportunity for professional learning. Without feedback, a professional cannot learn about the appropriateness of the original diagnosis of need, and referral. Further, a professional may have to continue to work with a client following a referral to another profession or service and lack of information about a client's progress may lead to a dangerous confusion, or overlap of effort.

The role of medical staff and medical information in multi-professional assessment of special educational needs causes concern for both medical staff and teachers and others who feel that they need access to medical advice and information (Wedell, Welton and Vorhaus 1981, Welton 1982). The circulars of guidance to local authorities on the provision of medical, psychological and educational advice for decision making about maintaining a 'Statement of Educational Need' under the 1981 Education Act reflect the sensitivity of the Department of Education and Science, and Department of Health and Social Services to this area of professional ethics.

The stratification of the welfare professions is most clearly illustrated in the way information is shared, but it should be noted that there is also a reluctance to share confidential information within the same profession until trust is fully established between peers. In recent research, a medical professional described to the author how within his branch of the school medical service, care was taken informally to assess the professional competence and acceptability of new colleagues before taking them fully into confidence. Sharing medical information outside the medical service was regarded as very difficult. The education service was regarded as very unprofessional in its handling of confidential information, although the doctor felt that it would be safe to give information to a chief educational psychologist because that person 'was a graduate'!

The value of professionalism lies in the maintenance of standards of service and in the protection of the client. Its dysfunctional aspects are found in protectionist behaviour which may at times appear to be as much concerned with maintaining the status of the profession as in protecting the interest of the client.

The blockages to cooperation and communication between schools and other parts of the welfare network can be overcome in various ways. Firstly by raising the general professional sensitivity to the need for collaboration and joint action to meet childrens needs. Demonstrating how by working with other professions, a social worker, medical doctor, or teacher can provide much more effectively for their client's needs. Secondly, through the development of informal contacts between members of each profession and service. Thirdly, through the development of formal systems of welfare coordination at policy making, administrative and professional levels.

It is not sufficient for teachers, social workers and others to wait until a crisis is imminent or has occurred before establishing communication with another agency. Effective multi-professional work requires understanding and trust built up over long period. The development of multi-professional cooperative care teams at both school and district levels are important ways of establishing good working relationships between schools and other welfare services (Welton 1982).

Regrettably the roots of distrust within the welfare network can lie very deep, even affecting the choice of profession in the first instance. As illustration, the author a few years ago had to meet the senior officer in charge of a regional welfare service to discuss research access to that service. Before he would discuss the research proposal, the senior officer talked for nearly an hour about his own school experience and how it still affected his expectations of teaching professionals. Parents, and even the most self-assured members of other welfare professions approach schools conscious of their own experience as pupils. Teachers may hold similar feelings about medical practitioners, and other members of the welfare professions.

Such anecdotes are not mere gossip, but illustrate the feelings which have to be overcome if successful coordination of services is to be achieved. Although this chapter has dwelt on some of the difficulties in establishing an effective multi-professional welfare network including schools, it is also based on a vision of cooperative care which is reflected in a number of recent trends in both welfare policy and professional practice.

Firstly the development of cooperative care teams in various schools and local areas reflects the extended professionalism of teachers, and the realization that formal and permanent liaison procedures are necessary. Communication between welfare sectors and professionals can not be left to chance, or to the informal linkages which develop between concerned people. Such informal linkages may be lost as key people move or change roles within a school or service.

Secondly, the development of welfare specialisms within schools such as the school counsellor, the training of tutors, and the development of home-school liaison is an indication of the increased attention which is being paid to welfare matters in school management.

Thirdly, official policy making is increasingly taking account of the need for inter-sectoral planning and implementation. The new legislation for special education in England and Wales, and the Black Committee Report on legislation for children and young people in Northern Ireland are good examples (Welton 1982, 1983).

The vision of effective multi-professional work to meet the needs of children and families involves both structural change and a cultural revolution!

Notes

1 This chapter is based on research, part published and part unpublished. A full account of the relationships described are to be published in a book by Heinemann.
2 The term 'profession' is used in this chapter to include all the non-administrative and non-technical staff offering a service to children and their families which includes a diagnosis of educational, social or medical need, and the ability to supply that need through the application of knowledge and skills obtained through training. It is not the purpose of this chapter to enter in the erudite, if sterile debate about whether certain occupations have a right to professional status, although as I have argued elsewhere the welfare network cannot be understood without a recognition of the problems which arise from its social stratification. Not all the welfare professions are accorded the same status either by lay people, or members of other welfare professions.

Schooling and Welfare: Taking Account of the Views and Feelings of Pupils

Peter Lang
University of Warwick

Introduction

Schools and teachers in many parts of the world can claim, with some justification, that they have a concern for the care of their pupils which extends beyond their cognitive development. Thus the United States, Canada and New Zealand have a long history of the employment of trained and specialist counsellors in educational institutions of all kinds and in Japan almost every secondary school contains Seitoshido-Shunin ('Heads of Pupil Personal Work'). Furthermore, in Britain and in countries as diverse as Australia, Jamaica, Nigeria, Israel and The Cayman the concept of 'pastoral care' has been widely used and institutionalized in a wide variety of structures, processes and activities (Lang and Ribbins, 1985).

Whilst the kind of concern identified above seems real it may also be rooted in over-simplified and stereotyped conceptions of the non-academic needs of children and of the understandings which pupils actually have of the purposes and functioning of the structures and processes designed to give that concern an organizational expression. If this should be the case it would not be surprising and can in part be explained by the fact that teachers, educationalists and social researchers have all given so little attention to how pupils construe their own caring and welfare needs and how they understand, interpret and work the systems and structures which schools have set up to meet what they see as the needs of pupils in this area. (See Lang, 1977, 1982; Best *et al.*, 1977, 1980, 1983.)

In this chapter I shall attempt to say something about the ways in which pupils actually do 'see' their own welfare and caring needs and how they understand the systems and processes which schools have set up to meet what teachers and others think these needs are. To undertake this task I will draw upon the scant literature which deals with this theme and will draw especially on a piece of on-going research in which I have been engaged for the last few years.

The Literature

There is a growing literature that deals with various aspects of the role of care and welfare in schools (Ribbins and Best, 1985). But little of it deals with the views of the pupils. Thus, for example, whilst Johnson *et al* (1980) devotes a whole chapter of *Secondary Schools and the Welfare Network* to the perspectives of teachers only a very few passing references are made to the views of pupils. Much the same could be said about the work of Craft (1980), Haigh (1975), Marland (1974) and of many others. Even where a writer has pointed to critical differences between pupil perceptions and those of teachers or other adults in schools, as in the case of Murgatroyd's (1977) study of pupil perceptions of school counsellors, such studies are usually isolated and have rarely prompted further investigation.

None of this has prevented the development of a variety of competing accounts, rooted in different ideologies as to what are the characteristic problems which young people face and how these problems are to be explained. A continuum of explanations might be identified with towards one polar extreme, accounts, which stress factors related to individuals and their development as a crucial source of such problems (Erickson, 1950; Moser, 1975), and towards the other extreme, explanations which emphasise external factors related to the economic and social structures of society and their implications for pupils in schools (Corrigan, 1979; Robins and Cohen, 1978; Willis 1980).

Whatever the considerable merits of these and similar models three related points can be made about them. First, used in isolation, they do not offer adequate explanations of the causes of young people's problems and are, in any case usually based on limited empirical evidence. Secondly, they are often espoused in schools for reasons that have little to do with their inherent validity. Finally, they may *all* deflect attention away from the school itself as a possible source of problems (Lang, 1982).

Another kind of problem with the assumptions which some

schools make about meeting the welfare needs of their pupils is a tendency to exaggerate the significance of the contribution made by the activities of their own or of wider welfare systems and networks. This assumption is shared in some of the relevant literature although there are also cases to the contrary which stress, for example, the crucial role of peer group (Kitwood, 1980) or of family (MacBeth, 1985) support. How schools perceive these kinds of issues will significantly shape what they do.

Much of this points to the needs for schools to articulate what might be described as a *'world view'* to shape their ideas and actions. Certainly, my own research and that of others suggests that pupils will have their own 'world views' and that, during times of recession in particular, such views are likely to be pessimistic. If teachers have no alternatives to offer it is hard to see how they can engage in relevant welfare interaction with their pupils. If this is so, then schools and teachers will have to be clear on where they stand on such issues as expressed in the current debates on the purposes of schooling as an educational, vocational or training preparation for life.

In this preliminary section of my paper I have only been able to identify some of the issues which I see as significant and to sketch out in the briefest way some of their implications. To an extent what I have argued is that schools and teachers must be clearer about what they see as the purposes of their welfare-orientated activities than they often are at present. I shall now go on to argue that such a clarification, whilst in some sense prior to the need to be clear about how pupils construe their own needs and how they understand the systems schools set up to meet these needs, should not be seen as all that is needed. Rather, schools and teachers, if they are to make effective welfare provision for their pupils, must understand how the latter see these things themselves.

Pupils Perspectives on their Welfare Needs and upon the Provision made for this in Schools

Perforce, much of what I have to say on this topic will be drawn from my own researches into this theme. My research has had two main aspects. The first took the form of a detailed, case study of the pastoral care system of a large comprehensive school in the West Midlands (Lang, 1982). From this research I distinguished the existence of a 'conventional wisdom' held by many teachers characterized by a belief that they knew: (1) How pupils construed their own welfare needs; (2) How pupils understood the schools pastoral systems and activities. This confidence was expressed in the kinds of things they said. Thus one house head remarked that 'when you have been here as long as I have, you know very well what their (the pupils) problems are', and a tutor commented that 'we take a lot of trouble about induction in this school, the vast majority of the pupils have an excellent understanding of the system from the outset as a result of this work'. However, little attempt has been made to test the validity of such judgments and the views of pupils were largely taken for granted. The second aspect of my research has focused upon a questionnaire-based study undertaken, as before, in the west Midlands, with responses from 250 pupils in twenty schools. This was followed up by thirty semi-structured interviews with a range of pupils in four of the twenty schools mentioned above (see Lang 1983, 1985). In this chapter I shall focus upon three main aspects of the perceptions of pupils to the welfare systems and activities which existed in the schools they attended — these aspects have to do with 'understandings', 'feelings' and 'problems'.

Pupils and their Understanding of Pastoral Systems and Pastoral Roles

How well do pupils understand the systems, structures and roles which schools have set up to meet their welfare needs? Given the range of schools in my sample, generalizations will need to be made with some caution as wide variations might be expected. In some schools there may be little to understand as was the case with one small high school I considered. Here there were teachers designated as 'house heads' but they seemed to be engaged in little that would be considered as 'pastoral' as the term is understood today. In other schools the teachers seemed to be scarcely less confused than their pupils — I found this to be quite common in schools which had introduced a programme of tutorial work without adequate staff preparation.

Two generalizations I feel I can make with some confidence. First, that teachers quite commonly believe that pupils do have an adequate grasp of their school's pastoral structures. Second, that this belief is all too often not particularly well founded. In fact, few pupils had any developed concept of a system or network designed to help them, more usually seeing the school's welfare activities in terms of the attitudes and activities of individual teachers regarded as persons rather than as the representatives of system. Typical comments were 'Mr. Hughes understands', 'You can talk to Mr. Carter', with remarks such as 'We have houses to help the teachers look after us' or 'its the tutors job to look after you' being much less common. Where pupils did have a notion of a system, they often saw individual teachers as supportive but the system as having an essentially disciplinary or administrative function. Some pupils showed awareness of the tensions inherent in such a situation as in the following observation by a fourth year boy: 'I think the house heads want to help us but they don't get a lot of time . . . they have a lot to sort out . . . so really they don't get much chance . . . some are sad about this'.

Many pupils described the two *key pastoral roles*, in a relatively favourable way. Both house/year heads and tutors were often described as being concerned with helping you with problems, sorting things out for you and seeing that you were fairly treated. 'His job (year head) is to see it from your point of view. He helps you with problems, sometimes he helps you with unfair teachers' (third year girl). However their general view of teachers was that care or concern for the welfare of individual pupils was not among their major concerns. As a third year boy put it: 'Teachers have to be mainly concerned about exam results'. It seemed that at this level pupils distinguished clearly between teachers in their pastoral role and in their class teacher role.

In my discussion with pupils and with those teachers particularly involved in pastoral care in schools quite substantial differences sometimes emerged as to how much pupils felt they had sought *support and help* from those involved in pastoral care and how much the staff themselves felt they had. This difference could be in either direction. In some cases pupils who felt they sought help a great deal were described to me by staff as rarely, if ever, using the system, equally in some cases pupils who I was told by staff were constantly seeking help felt they used the system only rarely. We should, perhaps, not be too surprised by this. A central focus of my research has been the understanding and clarification of the different levels of meanings which operate in schools at official and unofficial levels and at the level of statement and of action. It is essential that schools evaluating or developing their pastoral welfare provision should analyze and make explicit such differences.

Much of my research data suggested that the extent to which pupils understood teachers varied very much from individual to individual — some pupils having only the vaguest idea of the sort of things that concern and motivate teachers, while others, from all age groups, showed a much more developed and sophisticated understanding. Though the way pupils perceived and described the pastoral/welfare provision of their schools and the teachers involved in its administration, appears to have become generally more favourable during the four year period of my research into pupil perspectives, there was also evidence to suggest that the dialectic between care and control (Lang, 1984) and the over-emphasis on administration found in the structure and operation of pastoral care/welfare in a number of schools, (Best, Jarvis, Ribbins, 1977, 1980, 1983; Lang, 1977, 1980) has a significant effect on the way pupils perceive and understand this provision. In relation to this, many pupils felt that one of the central functions of the pastoral/welfare structures was image building as many of them put in; 'making sure the school keeps its good name.'

Feelings

How do pupils feel about their school's pastoral/welfare provision? Though considerable data relating to this area was collected, assessing and making sense of it was complicated by two factors. As has already been said, many pupils do not have a developed notion of a system but see things only in terms of the actions and attitudes of individual teachers. It may well be therefore that the feelings pupils described were not based on any long term experiences in relation to the school's provision but simply on a recent experience of a particular teacher.

The other complication was that the data indicated that most pupils had a notion of the way they would like things to be and the teachers they would like to have (that is, ones who stopped and helped you when you needed it — had a sense of humour, treated you like a human being and not just another pupil, etc.). However it was also clear that for most pupils things were often not like that. A number of the teachers they experienced were in many ways not the kind they liked. In the words of a fourth year girl 'A lot of teachers in this school push us too hard and nag too much', and of a fifth year girl 'I wouldn't tell Mrs Jones anything she tells other teachers, she's a blabber mouth'. Thus it was sometimes hard when pupils responded to questions such as 'What are the most important things about your house/year head's job?' or 'What are the most important things about your tutor's job?' to be sure that their answers reflected the way their year/house heads and tutors actually were or whether they were offering an idealized notion of the way they thought they ought to be. However it was still clear from the responses to these questions that, whilst some pupils would like their teachers to be more caring many other pupils viewed their house/year heads and tutors quite favourably and often identified as important, aspects that would be seen as central to these pastoral roles. Perhaps the most significant of these was the number of times pupils mentioned qualities closely connected with sympathy and understanding, fairness and preparedness to listen to your point of view as important for both their house/year heads and tutors. House/year heads were quite often identified with 'helping us with problems' and tutors with 'making sure that the groups get on together'. Equally, aspects of discipline and control and administration were often mentioned as was inter-group competitiveness.

When talking to pupils about the teachers in their schools, they liked and *trusted*, I found a number of significant variations. A few pupils said they liked and trusted all the teachers they came into contact with, though there were none who didn't have problems with one or two of their teachers. There were also a small number who claimed not to like or trust any of their teachers. However, most said they liked and trusted between three to six teachers. Further discussion generally revealed that those they liked and those they trusted were not necessarily the same people. Many pupils trusted teachers they didn't particularly like and some teachers they liked they didn't trust. This finding seems particularly worth further investigation as it is contrary to most assumptions about the types of relationships essential for effective pastoral care. Both questionnaire and interview research made it clear that aspects of confidence and trust are a key issue for a number of pupils. Strong feelings of resentment were expressed in a number of cases where it was felt a teacher had broken trust or confidence. My evidence has indicated that some schools and a fair number of teachers were either unaware of or insensitive to pupils' feelings in this area. It hardly needs saying that the development of an effective pastoral welfare provision in any school cannot ignore the types of feeling described.

Another significant variable in pupil feelings involved what they saw as legitimate concerns for their school. Feelings ranged from some pupils who felt that virtually any problem they were confronted with both in and out of the school was the school's business to those who felt that almost nothing to do with them was any of the school's concern. The majority of pupils however had clear ideas about those problems and concerns they might have which were the school's concern and those which weren't. Where they saw the dividing line varied quite considerably. Such divisions would make an excellent basis for discussion as part of a tutorial or pastoral programme — for example most pupils saw how they got on with their peers as the school's business, while how they got on with their brothers and sisters (often in the same school) as no business of the school.

Often pupils' *feelings* about school and their experience were reflected in an indirect way, for example in their comments about what made a good teacher — sense of humour, having a joke were frequently mentioned — as were treating you as a human being and stopping and helping you when you needed it. The frequency that both the last two comments were made suggest that this was often not what pupils experienced. Overall the research suggested a situation where for some pupils many teachers and lessons left them feeling rushed and confused — both in terms of not having enough time — and not enough help. Amongst the things pupils liked about school, the most often mentioned was that it was a place you met your friends. Though this may appear obvious, it is something not always recognized or taken account of in the ways schools are organized or respond to pupils. Many of the major dislikes that pupils expressed about their schools were strong feelings about relatively trivial administrative factors, for example, toilets that were mostly locked and when they weren't, were smelly and had no proper paper. Irritations that it often seemed quite possible for schools to remedy. Just over half the pupils involved in my research felt their last year at school had either been 'very happy' or 'happy', about forty per cent felt it had been 'alright', and just under ten per cent felt it had been 'miserable'.

When it came to pupils feelings about what the school should be doing for them, the vast majority were mainly concerned that it should get them a job and prepare them for a world which for most appeared bleak, hard and insensitive.

I have outlined above some of the pupil feelings apparent in their responses to my questions. These are significant at three distinct levels. First at a general level they show that an important and mainly unexamined dimension exists to our understanding of pastoral/welfare provision in schools. Second at the level of individual schools a greater awareness of the precise nature of pupil feelings will certainly influence the way a particular school organizes its provision. Finally, the utilitarian view of education and perceptions of the outside world as a bleak relentless place must have implications for the way the school formulates and presents its own world view.

Problems

That many pupils are confronted by a range of problems during their time at school is something that most teachers would not deny, though they might disagree on the nature, effect and relevance of these problems. There certainly would be some disagreement as to how much these problems were the concern of schools and teachers. As has already been suggested what is equally likely is that in most schools the notions which teachers hold of the kind of problems pupils commonly have, are based usually upon commonsense rather than upon any substantial and systematic evidence. How do pupils see their problems?

I have already suggested the problems which pastoral/welfare systems have responded to in the past and in some cases still tend to respond to are those which are first problems for teachers and schools and only secondly for pupils — indeed some could be seen as not problems for pupils at all; truancy, disruptive behaviour and disaffection could be seen as examples of this. At the very least what pupils have said has shown that the situation as regards the problems they encounter is more complex than is generally recognized. Their responses demonstrated that the range of problems that pupils feel they encounter, is very wide and that within this range the experience of individual pupils can be very different indeed. Some of the problems frequently mentioned were amongst those traditionally recognized by the pastoral care of most schools; bullying, difficulty with work, anxiety about employment; again other aspects mentioned equally often were not. How you and your friends got on together, reconciling social and school life, personality clashes with particular teachers. Amongst the things mentioned, their relationships with their peers and particularly their friends were very significant. Not surprisingly worries about future employment and getting a job loomed large amongst most pupils concerns, and this was not only amongst those towards the end of their school careers. Of obvious significance to schools is the fact that the type of problem mentioned by far the most frequently by pupils, were those generated by aspects of the schools themselves, either in terms of their organization or of the approach, attitude and demands of their teachers. There is no doubt that the problems traditionally associated with welfare and pastoral provision, such as social background, poverty, over-crowding, unemployment and single parent families, are on any criteria significant and it's right that a considerable amount of pastoral work should focus on them. Nevertheless, in terms of pupils' perceptions of the things that are problems for them, these more traditional concerns do not figure very significantly. I am not suggesting that school's pastoral welfare responses should be organized solely on the basis of pupils own perceptions, but I do believe that in the development and maintenance of an effective pastoral welfare provision an understanding of pupils' perceptions of the things that seem to them to be problems must be an important dimension. If they do have problems, who do they seek help from?

Who pupils said they could or would go to when they had problems raised some important difficulties which would warrant further investigation. The central one being that though many pupils had reasonably favourable views of those in pastoral roles, when asked who they would go to about a range of problems, some of which were very clearly related to aspects of school — too much homework, teachers picking on them, not understanding the work, having no friends in your group — teachers were not often mentioned. Parents, relatives and peers were mentioned more often for almost every type of problem. Given this, does not the perception which schools and teachers all too often have of the family — as a generator of problems for pupils — need revision? Rather than seeing the school's main task as compensating for family problems, should not attempts be made to work in cooperation with the family conceiving of it as the kind of parallel pastoral system suggested by Alastair Macbeth (1985). Another implication is that a greater understanding is needed of the actual process by which pupils seek help from schools and individual teachers and precisely how they feel about this.

How pupils feel about the problems they have, the things that worry them most, the very wide range of different problems which affect different individuals amongst any group of pupils, and the role the school plays in the creation of many of these problems, have all been discussed in this section and are all things that it would be valuable for those involved in the school's welfare/pastoral provision to understand more clearly. What can we learn from all this?

Implications and Questions

The sometimes contradictory nature of pupil responses outlined in the preceding sections of this chapter raises questions about the exact significance that can be attached to the views and feelings that pupils express and the precise relationship between different facets of their perceptions as they describe them. For example, their responses indicate that they see teachers in general as relatively unconcerned about care yet they often describe those in pastoral middle management and tutorial roles as caring and understanding. These two perceptions must on some occasions be of the *same teacher*. Do these apparently conflicting views reflect confusion on the part of pupils or alternatively an awareness of the different facets of the teacher's role? Though they appear to recognize that there are people concerned with helping with problems in their school and they regularly mention having been helped by them, when asked who they would go to with a range of problems these people are hardly mentioned. What pupils do mention, however, are the many problems schools create for them, yet they also describe their last year at school as happy. Those things most traditionally associated with the school's welfare provision and clearly of considerable significance — poverty, poor diet, single parent families, unemployed parents — feature very little in pupils' comments. Certainly and not very surprisingly the investigation of a previously almost unexamined area while increasing understanding has also raised a new range of questions that may need to be answered by further research.

One question that was asked of the data was, do pupils' perspectives vary according to the school which they attend? The evidence suggests that they do but not always in the way that might have been expected. For example, I could detect no major difference between pupils' views in one relatively relaxed and progressive school I visited and another where the head claimed to run 'a tight ship' and in fact did so. It seems to be the attitude of the teachers and more subtle aspects of the school's ethos that influence pupils rather than educational philosophy and management style, though of course all these are closely related. One implication of the material presented and arguments outlined in this paper relates to the notion of a pastoral curriculum — if schools are to take this conception of the schools' pastoral/welfare provision seriously, and it is increasingly clear that they should do, information on the kinds of problems pupils have is something they will need to be aware of. Most writers on the pastoral curriculum (Marland, 1980; Mclaughlin, 1983) suggest that the preventative nature of such a curriculum means that a central focus must be on the potential problems that the majority of pupils will encounter. To arrive at any valid view of this, it is essential that the perspectives of pupils be taken into account in the process of making decisions about their welfare needs and in the discussion and decisions about how these needs are to be met.

I believe that the kind of approach discussed above will have far reaching implications for schools and for teachers which must be recognized from the outset. It is not only concerned with the way we view pupils and the systems we claim to have set up to serve them but also with problems of how we involve them, both in terms of sampling their attitudes and also actively in terms of helping decide what sort of system there is and what are the things that are actively covered. The development of such an approach is likely to raise two further issues. Just how far can schools go, firstly in terms of what they can tolerate — there are clearly limits to the extent to which even the most assured and democratic teacher will go in terms of pupils' involvement in decisions, the forcing through of a programme of pupils involvement in a way that is against the wishes of most staff and seen by them as threatening, is not likely to be successful.

The other issue is, how well teachers handle these added insights. There is already a fair amount of evidence, some from my own data, that at present teachers do not always really know how to make use of insights about pupils in a way which is beneficial to them and that they can handle confidentiality badly. These issues require in themselves real discussion and analysis in schools and also school-based in-service training.

Response and Action

A number of responses by schools are proposed or implied in my paper. I shall now comment on the most central of these. Firstly, any individual school which is concerned to act positively must re-examine the world view/ideology that underpins its current practice — even if this actually involves the establishment of the lack of a coherent one. This must not only be made explicit but may well need modifying. For example, in relation to the pupils' own world view. The need for such reviews will be even more pressing with the increasing involvement of parents at a policy-creating level in schools.

A less fundamental but valuable response would be the development of frameworks to assist in the analysis, location and understanding of problems. An example of such a framework might be in terms of the contexts from which problems originate. Contexts might be focused upon the individual, the peer group, the school and more broadly environmental/cultural in their location. This could be developed to: problems orignating from individual development, emotional deprivation etc.; problems originating from interpersonal relations and the operation of groups; problems originating from the nature of institutions, the family, the school; problems originating from aspects of social background, social differentiation, race, sex, class etc; problems originating from cultural and material disadvantage.

My discussion had already made it clear that how teachers and pupils located major problems within such a framework would often be different. Attempts to develop such an analysis by a school might not only promote greater understanding of the nature of pupil problems and the refinement of the pastoral/welfare system, the individual and preventitive pastoral curricula response, but also help to close the gap between teachers and pupils' perceptions of the nature and location of the problems.

As has already been suggested, schools will need to develop strategies for involving pupils, there are clearly a number of ways they might do this which it is not the purpose of this chapter to discuss in detail, the range stretches from informal discussion, discussion with groups of pupils, through semi-structured interviews with a representative sample to systematically devised and administered questionnaires. Schools may choose to use their own staff, or ask an experienced outsider to act as researcher. Some schools may prefer to build such sampling into their formal curricula activities for example, as part of a social studies course — or again where a school has a formalized pupil representation structure, schools councils etc, the sampling might be undertaken through this. Such developments should mean a valuable extension of both pastoral middle managers and tutors roles as, however undertaken, they should be involved in both aspects; a review of pupil perspectives on the welfare/pastoral provision of the school and the involvement of pupils within it.

Finally, schools should not allow such an investigation to focus on problems alone, there are positive and developmental aspects to pupil perspectives, what they enjoy about school, what they like about teachers. It is essential that a balance within the welfare/pastoral provision is maintained between problems and positive development and enjoyment.

Conclusion

In this paper I have suggested that pupils perspectives and feelings in relation to pastoral care and welfare are very much more complex and significant than is usually appreciated. Schools need to examine pupils' view and in relation to this to clarify and unpack the assumption made about the views and needs of pupils which under-pin their own practice. Having done this the ground is prepared for real development and progress. What exactly this will mean for each individual school is not the subject of this chapter, though it will clearly mean as much work and thought as will have gone into progressing through the work described in the main body of this paper. For it's not enough to increase our understanding and awareness, it's knowing what to do with increased understanding and awareness.

Parents, Schooling, and the Welfare of Pupils*

Michael Marland
Headmaster North Westminster Community School,
ILEA and Honorary Professor of Education,
University of Warwick

Introduction: Welfare Needs

It could well be argued that the most important thing schooling can do for the 'welfare' of pupils is to teach them the concepts, attitudes, facts, and skills that they will need to use to control their future environment, and thus ensure their own welfare. Indeed the success of all aspects of the curriculum of a school is essential to a pupil's whole 'welfare'. Whilst I agree with that, such a large concept of 'welfare', virtually synonymous with 'education', is so broad and unfocused that it does not allow the theorist or the practitioner to consider aspects of technique and procedure and so sharpen them for the good of the pupil.

Further, the 'learning' of pupils is considerably handicapped in most instances if their welfare is poor. The child who is faring well in 'health, prosperity, and well being' is likely to be (but one can say little more with certainty) better able to take up the role of the pupil (Bazlegette, 1983) and use the school for her or his benefit.

It is useful to consider what elements make up a child's 'welfare', and to consider the role of the school in working with parents to enhance that state. I am defining 'welfare' as the physical health, clothing and equipping, 'chaperonage' (Harriet Wilson's phrase for

---

* Some sections of this chapter derive from a paper I did for the EEC for the conference, 'The school and the family in the European Community', 1982, and subsequently printed in a revised and shortened form in the *Westminster Studies in Education*, 17, 1984.

the supervision offered by guardians and parents) mental health, attendance, and attitude of a pupil. Many aspects of a child's welfare are the commonplace of parenting, and it is easy in schools to forget how much parenting effort has been required to establish the basics of health, sleep, safety, clothing, and parental love and support.

Whilst it would probably be agreed that the prime responsibility for the welfare in that definition of the child lies with those who care for it at home, the school has a dual responsibility: (a) to use its educational skills, range of activities, and unique knowledge of the child to *facilitate* and *amplify* the work of parents, and (b) to *complement* that parental work when necessary.

Sometimes the welfare needs of a child will be so acute that specific professional help is imperative: medical, psychiatric, housing, legal, or financial. In those cases, as I discuss later, the school's main task with parents is to help them seek and accept that specific professional help. In the large majority of cases, though, the child's welfare needs are well within the norm of most other children. In the wisest and most comprehensive study of children with psychiatric difficulties written for all of us dealing with children, Michael Rutter makes the fundamental point of all welfare issues:

> The next point that arises from epidemiological research is that, for the most part, the disorders do *not* constitute diseases or illnesses which are *qualitatively* different from normality. There are a few conditions such as infantile autism, which might be termed diseases in this sense, but this is not true of the great majority of disorders. Most conditions differ *quantitatively* from the normal in terms both of severity and of associated impairment, but minor variations of the same thing can be found in many essentially normal children. (Rutter, 1975, p. 17)

In this continuum of needs, it is vital not to overlook the welfare needs of *all* children in our worry about the major difficulties. I sometimes argue gloomily that most pupils don't receive pastoral care as they don't appear to have severe enough 'problems'! This emphasis on the serious problem is one of the biggest weaknesses of our pastoral care work. Sometimes it is almost as if only those pupils with one or more of a certain list of problems are deemed as requiring care. Parents feel this:

> Teachers were themselves contributing towards an expecta-
> tion that at parents' evening they only wished to discuss

problems. Many parents reported teachers saying to them, 'You're not the parents we want to see, the parents we need to see are the ones that never come', implying that they wanted to see the parents of children with problems, so as to discuss those problems at the parents' evening. (Johnson and Ransom, 1983, p. 56)

All children have some needs, and there will be times when the sensitive teacher at school will perceive these and be able to draw parents' attention to them, and on other occasions this will be reversed. An experienced school social worker, Karen Lyon, has analyzed 184 referrals to her as an 'education social worker'. Twenty-nine per cent she defined as 'social problems' ('relationships within the family, and/or concern about the care of the child'); twenty-nine per cent were 'behavioural problems'; nineteen per cent 'educational'; thirteen per cent 'medical'; and ten per cent 'attendance'. (Lyon, 1980, p. 240)

What can schools hope to do *with* parents about this range of problems? It is often more use to the pupil to help her or him work on the surface symptoms than to explore the multifactorial *causes*. With most presentations of welfare needs the search for 'the cause' is counter-productive and anyway unnecessary. Rutter elsewhere makes a similar point about psychiatric disorders:

> In general psychiatry, at least in the past, there has been a tendency to use the same model. Diagnoses such as schizophrenia or manic-depressive psychoses also imply a disease or illness and researchers are carrying out investigations to determine *the* cause of these diseases. To some degree this framework is applicable to a few of the rare psychiatric disorders in childhood, but it is not appropriate for the majority of commoner disorders. The disorders are not diseases — psychiatric problems have many facets not easily encompassed in a single term, and typically the disorders are multifactorily determined. It does not make sense to search for *the* cause for there are usually several. (*ibid*, p. 25)

The school is usually more profitably engaged working *with* parents to find ways of helping the pupil adjust current aspects of behaviour.

Every school I've known has cared for the welfare of its pupils, but very often it is through a barrier of misunderstandings about parents, and as a result at the best the work has been slowed up or made more awkward, and at the worst it has been made impossible.

The first step, therefore, must be to explore teachers' professional attitudes to the prime carers for children — parents and guardians.

Teachers' and School Attitudes

These responsibilities of the school are severely affected by the way we see parents. Our view is one inherited from the two great traditions of the past: schools are omnipotent and parents inadequate. Two real episodes, one from the past and one recent, epitomize these approaches:

1   Finding a young pupil weeping miserably, James Boyer, the famous nineteenth-century boarding-school Headmaster of Samuel Coleridge and Charles Lamb, questioned him. When he was told that the misery was because he missed his parents, Boyer declared: 'Boy! the *school* is your father! Boy! school is your mother ... and all the rest of your relations!' (Morpurgo, 1951, p. 113)
2   A few years ago a headteacher in Birmingham said of the West Indian pupils in the school: 'The parents are glad their children are getting an education, but they can't give much help ... they need to stop working shifts and see something of their kids'. (Rex and Tomlinson, 1979, p. 202)

These two authentic voices illustrate the often unspoken but always powerful complementary assumptions about schooling and parents in Britain: the first, lingering still from the nineteenth century, is that school is omnipotent, offering, as the boarding school endeavoured to, all the requirements for a full life; the second, sharply felt by the many teachers unsure of their own social background and current status, is that parents do not care, and are incompetent to 'support' their children's education. I have frequently met unwarranted criticism, resentment, patronizing condescension, and sheer blindness to the real attitudes of parents. In schools in 'difficult' inner-city areas the pressures of teaching can lead to a gross undervaluing of parents. One otherwise excellent, experienced, and likeable professional teacher said to a whole staff meeting: 'These parents don't deserve such good teachers'! Baroness Warnock gave fresh life to these old stereotypes in 1985 in the BBC Dimbleby Lecture when she labelled her perceptions of parents as being 'pushy' or 'apathetic' (Warnock 1985).

The received opinion amongst many teachers is that the working class child is disadvantaged at school partially at least because of weak parental interest in schooling in general and the child's educational progress: Douglas in 1964 (Douglas, 1964) and the Plowden Committee three years later (Central Advisory Council, 1967) in its own research claimed a very strong association between educational achievement and parental attitudes to school. These findings have become educational commonplaces even amongst those who have read neither source. However, later commentators have seen the measures that these researchers used as indicators of parental interest rather as manifestations of class behaviour, and Acland (1980) worked through the Plowden data afresh. The essence of his findings is that the variables most closely identified with parental involvement did not correlate strongly with achievement. Mortimore and Blackstone (1982, pp. 48–52) discuss the arguments comprehensively, and conclude:

> The evidence on parental interest, or lack of it, needs to be treated with caution. Sometimes at least part of the evidence is based on indicators which may not be the most sensitive or even the most appropriate and which may be measuring something other than parental interest . . . It seems likely that there are several possible explanations for behaviour which is often interpreted as lack of interest. (Mortimore and Blackstone, 1982, p. 52)

As Barbara Tizard and Martin Hughes pointed out, there is a 'general belief that mothers, as educators, have very little to offer'. They suggest that: 'This attitude may be partly due to the lowly, non-professional status which parenting is given.' (Tizard and Hughes, 1984, p. 17) In the nursery context they studied on most counts the girls in many ways learnt more at home than at school in all social classes! For instance: 'The school's curriculum was, in fact, considerably narrower than the home's — a smaller range of topics was discussed.' (Tizard and Hughes, 1984, p. 183.)

Few substantial attempts have been made to establish what parents actually feel and think. Perhaps the major English study is that of the 'Schools, parents, and social services project' funded by the English and Welsh Department of Education and Science between 1974 and 1977 (Johnson, *et al.*, 1980). This research contradicted completely the school-teacherly fallacies that there are a few enthusiastic regularly attending parents, a minority of 'problem parents' (with whom schools also had considerable contact), and in between a huge uninterested, non-attending, apathetic, group of parents — whom teachers regard as virtually invisible. Johnson and her colleagues interviewed over a hundred parents from a cross-section of parents 'in modest circumstances'. Their findings are a major adjustment of the received wisdom of schools: parents had seen primary school as a weaning from home; they did not then want to reverse this. They themselves did not necessarily consider it right to curtail their children's activities, and did not therefore see it proper to interfere too much in school. They found it strange that teachers admitting to difficulties in handling teenagers should expect parents to wield undiminished authority over them! To many parents, the encounters with teachers appear as demands by the school for accounting for their parenting, or for mere support of the *school* as an institution.

Whereas teachers judged support only in terms of home-school links, parents saw home-based support for the youngster as very important — and gave it far more often than teachers realized. Often schools knew virtually nothing of the range of ways in which ordinary homes encouraged, supported, taught, and transported to classes or sports. Teachers were especially blind about the help given by older siblings, who were often able to give advice and encouragement that was far more acceptable than that from other sources.

Another study which focused on parents and schools in detail was the 'East Sussex' project in 1978 and 1979. Mainly concerned with 'accountability', it incorporated a close consideration of school-parent communication. Chapter 3, 'Parents and teachers', seems to me the best account of the present relationship between parents and teachers in this country, and its sympathetic analysis leads to easy suggestions for improvement. (Becher, *et al.*, 1981)

There is also a temptation to see the 'problems' of parents as the only begetter of the 'problems' of children. Parents find themselves blamed for the difficulties the teachers face. Studies of parents' evenings confirm this:

> The parents were more nervous about the event than the teachers realized. They felt they were being scrutinized by the teacher, and themselves held accountable for their child's performance. (Johnson and Ransom, 1983, p. 56)

Indeed, sometimes parents' evenings are virtually a handback, in which the teacher says in effect: 'We professionals who've been trained can't handle your son. Could you please over the next weekend change him so that we can cope more easily.' It is like saying: 'I've failed, now you do it — by remote control'!

Sadly, but not surprisingly, when a large sample of teachers was studied it was found that they 'defined their roles as to educate parents about school aims and practice, rather than to understand the parents' values and priorities' (Johnson and Ranson, 1983, p. 53).

Thus, the common phrases 'co-operative parents' or 'supportive parents' are usually synonyms for 'parents who see things our way'. Schools often are asking for their own perspective to be confirmed back to them. So the 'good parent' is one who agrees and supports. However, 'the supportive parent' is really one who supports their youngster, not necessarily the school, and a school who defines 'supportive' in such profession-centric rather than child-centric terms is unlikely to be able to work well with parents.

Ethnic Minority Families

If the average family can be daunted by school, ethnic minority families, who have often suffered financial and racial indignities, find schools very difficult to relate to. However, that very formulation implies that the problem lies in the parents, when it is in fact the school's task to resolve the problem. Such families can see the welfare concern of a school as patronizing intrusion, just another example of white middle-class superiority.

The attitudinal problems that most UK teachers have towards most families are even greater with ethnic minority families. Whilst communication with these families presents the same imperatives, offers the same problems, and requires the same kinds of professional techniques as with majority groups, it is not sufficient to work as if the school were 'colour blind'. There are special needs resulting from the underlying racism and the usually greater misunderstanding by schools of family life in ethnic minority groups. It seems to me that the presence of the ethnic minority families does not fundamentally change but certainly sharpens and reveals more clearly the problems and the needs.

I concur with the findings of the Birmingham study:

> The immigrant parents' expectations of the schools and the definition of their children as a problem, both by educational policy-makers and by teachers, produce a situation of mis-understanding at best and direct conflict at worst. (Rex and Tomlinson, 1979, p. 204)

An earlier study of *Organisation in Multi-Racial Schools* reported depressingly: 'In general, home-school relations appear to be one of the most unsatisfactory areas of life in multi-racial schools.' (Townsend, 1972, p. 89)

The need is heightened by the attainment differential in certain respects between ethnic groups at sixteen plus, as clearly shown in surveys in the Inner London Education Authority schools (Mortimore, 1981) and more generally of pupils of West Indian origin (Taylor, 1981; Committee of Inquiry, 1981). Of course, there are important caveats to these statistics (including the catching-up effect by black pupils who stay on at school longer [Rutter, 1982]). However, the perceived facts have two complementary serious effects on home-school communication: one is the bitterness in many parts of the West Indian community (Black People's Progressive Association, 1978; Coard, 1971). The other is the increased tendency for teachers to parody even the stereotypes of ethnic minority parents and family life. These two factors are the result of poor home-school understanding, and do a great deal of harm to the community, the school, and the progress of the pupils.

Teachers tend to blame the home, and interpret, for instance, lower attendance at parents' evenings (confirmed in Black People's Progressive Association, 1978; and Rex and Tomlinson, 1979) as signs of 'apathy' — a word I have heard too often in schools — and 'poor family circumstances'. Both need reconsidering. The evidence does *not* support 'apathy':

> Contrary to widespread beliefs that some minority group parents do not take much interest in their children's education, our study indicated that not only do they take great interest, but both West Indian and Asian parents have made particular efforts to try to understand a complex and unfamiliar system, and they have high expectations of school. (Tomlinson, 1980, pp. 188–9)

My experience of parents' meetings at North Westminster confirms that of the Rex study in Handsworth (Rex and Tomlinson, 1979) that 'Asian' parents are likely to include a rather high proportion of non-visitors to school. Their reasons, however, are *not* those of the apathetic; rather they are largely the practical problems of shift hours, language difficulties, and the fact that school is often the only major 'white' institution with which an Asian in an English city has to relate — for many Asian workers who have lived in England for many years work, shop and socialize almost wholly within their ethnic community. These factors combine with an attitude to schooling that leads them deliberately not to wish to 'interfere'. Rex and Tomlinson found, as I find weekly, *no* signs of apathy, indeed considerable evidence in most families of extreme concern.

Indeed, David Quinton's family studies and review of the research compellingly refutes many aspects of the stereotype (Quinton 1980, pp. 61–5). In the meantime, the split widens. As Maureen Stone says:

> While schools try to compensate children by offering Black Studies and steel bands, black parents and community groups are organizing Saturday schools — to supplement the second-rate education which the school system offers the parents. There is a mis-match between the system and the community. (Stone, 1981, p. 11)

Those of us responsible in schools must look to ourselves: our image, language, practical arrangements, attitudes, and knowledge. Each has to be improved if the links are to be improved. For instance, parents can be invited (in letters in the appropriate mother tongue) at time to suit themselves, and to bring a friend if they wish. The school might need to provide an interpreter. The onus must be on the professional to help the parents: that is our professional task.

It is depressing that a follow-up to the Townsend NFER study of multi-ethnic education (quoted earlier, Townsend, 1972) by the Schools Council in 1981 echoed the same weakness:

> Seventy per cent (of Local Education Authorities) commented that minority ethnic group parents were less active than white British parents in parent-teacher associations and the other forms of parental involvement. (Little and Wiley, 1981, p. 24)

A great deal depends on schools' finding ways of changing this situation rapidly. As it is, bilingual familes rarely get their full share of pastoral care effort, and English-speaking ethnic minority groups are grossly misunderstood.

I've come to label an attitude that lies in most of us and dominates in some as 'parentism' — that is presuming deficiences in people because they are parents. It is abundantly clear from the major research studies now available that not only are the huge majority of parents not apathetic but very concerned, but also that the nature of their concerns and the modes of their support have a great deal to teach us teachers. The school's concern for the welfare of its pupils and its anxiety to work as an enabler of parents and to complement their work is disastrously inhibited if its attitudes are inappropriate.

Michael Marland

Towards a School Programme for Families

If schools are to work successfully with parents for the interlocked aims of the learning and welfare of the children, the individual action by a teacher is much more likely to be successful if there is an overall school programme. I have itemized nineteen specific acts, activities, or policies which appear to be essential as a matrix of school/family links:

> *Components of a Programme*
> 1 Good, informative printed brochures.
> 2 Opportunities to visit and question the school in advance of school-placement decision.
> 3 Full induction and reception interviews for *both* parents or guardians (if there are two).

The Macbeth report gives a large number of useful practical details (Macbeth, 1984). Things are bound to go wrong from time to time. It is very difficult if that is the first time that both parents have met the teacher handling matters. In many communities, relating to school is left to the mother; in a few non-English speaking Asian families it is left almost entirely to the father (who usually has a better command of the school's language). Then the unknown parent suddenly makes contact himself or herself at a time of crisis — and there is no background of a more ordinary day-to-day relationship on which to build the present negotiations.

> 4 A clear and accurate procedure for noting and promulgating the correct spelling, form, and pronunciation of both the family's and the pupil's names.

Teachers educated in one culture and linguistic pattern are likely to find spelling, copying, and pronouncing of the names of many ethnic minority and immigrant families really quite difficult. Haste, thoughtlessness and ignorance (for example, over Muslim naming systems) all lead to a variety of mistakes — each one of which is hurtful at the least to a pupil.

> 5 Efficient and pleasant reception and waiting arrangements for visitors.
> 6 Reliable message-taking arrangements.
> 7 A regular and carefully used *Diary* system.

At North Westminster, as in some other schools, pupils use a specially printed *Diary* not only to note their homework and plan their time, but also as an easy means of home-school co-operation: the signature of every week is a quick exchange of satisfaction with the work, and any brief queries can be included (rather as Macbeth: 'Carnets de liaison', Macbeth, 1984, p. 49).

8   Specific letters home or special matters, including praise!
9   Home visiting, both routine and for special purposes.
10   Reports.

The Macbeth report has commented on the frequency and style of reports (with the UK 'showing a trend towards fewer but fuller reports', Macbeth, 1984, p. 51). I wish to stress only that report-writing is a difficult skill, and the technicalities of the format are of considerable importance in assisting good report-writing. The issue of how to grade pupil's work is technically very difficult. (I have written on both these points in Marland, 1974 Chapter 9; and North Westminster, 1981.) They have to be well written, objective, clear, encouraging, warm, and related to the possiblility of help by parents.

11   Demonstration lessons.

Although all the evidence is that most parents mostly want to hear about their own child's progress, information on what the curriculum and teaching are like is appreciated by many.

12   Parent consultation meetings — to discuss individual pro-
     gress.
13   Invitations to all quasi-public school events.
14   Courses on education.

General courses can be run for parents on the education of their children. For instance, in West Hailes Education Centre, a commu-nity school near Edinburgh, Scotland, a five-week course is run every school term: 'Parents, Children and Education'. 'This course is geared to educating parents about their children's education in WHEC. It is very informal and lasts for about five weeks. There will be one running each term.' (West Hailes Education Centre, 1982, p. 11)

15   Special Parent/Teacher social and cultural events.
16   Opportunities to join ordinary classes, or specially formed
     classes.
17   Opportunities for parental help.

The most effective partnership evidence has been when there has been a need for the professional and the lay parent to plan an agreed programme of specific co-operation to solve an acute problem. This can be seen most dramatically with medical or quasi-medical problems. For instance parents have been shown to be effective partners in the successful treatment of enuresis (Griffiths *et al.*, 1982). More encouraging for the ordinary teacher is the variety of ways in which parents of handicapped children have been able to work with their children under the guidance of the professionals on joint programmes. Gillian Pugh in *Parents as Partners* (Pugh, 1982) has described how the teachers' skills can be used to help the parents, who can then work with individual children more intensively than any professional teacher. In more ordinary circumstances similarly impressive results have been found in seeking parents' help with their children's reading, and it is not surprising that effective efforts to encourage parents to assist in children's reading have produced very encouraging results, but it is surprising how effective intervention can be. Tizard and her colleagues worked in six inner-city multi-racial schools in a very poor area and encouraged parents to give reading practice. Not only did the pupils with this specially engendered parental support do better than the control classes, but they did better than the pupils given small-group instruction by a highly competent specialist teacher. (Mortimore and Blackstone, 1982, review the work on pp. 131–3.) Even more surprising is the evidence that reading can be substantially helped by a parent listening to the child read *even if the parent has little or no command of the language of the book* (Tizard, *et al.* 1982)!

Although none of this research is necessarily evidence on the effect of parental involvement in different aspects of learning or at older ages, each example has one thing in common with that other generally successful example of parental involvement: instrumental music. Very few children succeed in learning a musical instrument if they have not got a parent or other adult who supervises the practise, sometimes directing the young player to specific exercises even if she or he is not able to play the instrument. In all these cases the general injunction to 'take an interest' can be more closely focused into the prompting, overseeing, and even participating with the children for very closely defined and clearly recognizable tasks, the value of which to progress is quite obvious to child and parent. Some experience of teachers' having been able to find similar tasks for other aspects of the secondary curriculum leads me to consider that parents could be effective teaching partners far more often if we teachers were able to work with the parents to define the tasks, and this is equally true of 'welfare' issues.

In all those cases, parents have been working in a partnership with professionals to help their own children. However, parents can also be partners in helping children more generally in the class at all ages. There is a certain amount of experience of this in some schools in England, but mainly with younger classes. Indeed in the English primary school the proportion of classes receiving parental help falls sharply as children get older, from thirty-one per cent of the classes of seven year olds, to eighteen per cent by eleven years of age (HMI, 1978, p. 35). Few secondary schools make adequate use of the knowledge and expertise of their parents for school subjects, careers, especially work trailing or shadowing (see Watts, 1983), and community experience.

18   Formal representation on any 'governing body' or 'school council' and a formal place in the consultation and decision-making of the school.

19   A conscious decision to look at the School's way of doing things from a parent's point of view.

Reception of New Pupils

If later collaboration with families is to work, the initial reception and induction must be sympathetically, meticulously, and energetically arranged. Parents or guardians (*both* if there are two, though too few schools arrange this) need to be met with the child, and full details gathered — from the precise addresses and phone numbers (including home, work, and 'contact') to general aspects of the family. Correct names (as wished for) need to be noted, and all the details of the pupil, including medical, dietary, religious, and other requests. Such a reception interview is fairly common, but by no means universal. It is a skilled art to make best use of that time and to learn as much as possible, recording it for others, and at the same time conveying a warm, understanding, and approachable view of the school.

The Education Welfare Officer

The only professional whose sole task is to link home and school is the Educational Welfare Officer. Her or his function, however, is hampered by two inherited difficulties:

(a)   The developments promised for the service didn't materialize, as its main historian writes:

It is only with the last decade, however, that this role has begun to receive increased public attention. For the previous hundred years, education welfare offiicers were left to develop their own expertise with neither public recognition nor support. Then came a flurry of government reports on education and the social services, which began to mention the education welfare service and its potential for further development. Working parties were set up and national research on the role was undertaken. It seemed that official recognition, better training, and career prospects were on the way. Yet to date this has not happened, except on a very modest scale and at the initiative of a few local authorities. (MacMillan, 1980, p. 217, and see also MacMillan, 1977)

(b) Teachers, lacking any coherent briefing, misunderstand their function, often referring too early simple matters (which a phone-call home or to parents' work would solve), or too late (if at all) on serious matters (over which the different professional stance and experience could be valuable).

The question of when to refer to the EWO is insufficiently debated. The welfare of more pupils should be discussed with the EWO and his or her advice sought, but whether it is teacher or EWO who takes action should be discussed. In some cases it is better if home contact is from the EWO, but there are other occasions when most contact should be from a teacher. Whatever is decided parents must be taken into the confidence of the school/EWO/partnership and parents or guardians know that there is indeed a partnership.

Baulking at Referrals

Many outside services appear threatening to parents, and indeed from the point of view of parents and guardians, educational welfare officers and educational psychologists, for instance, *are* threatening in that they challenge parenting and in some way and to some extent take over part of that parenting role. However, the acceptability or otherwise of referral and of the other professional or institution is not merely dependent on the alleged 'reasonableness' or otherwise of the individual parent. Rather there are a number of factors under the influence of the professionals that can help make the parents more or less willing to consider the referral hopefully:

(a) *Previous school-family relationship:* If the suggestion that one's son requires referral to an educational psychologist comes after months without communication or a series of unpleasant ones, the suggestion of referral is likely to be resisted. *Successful referral requires a previous history of successful communication.*

(b) *Previous discussion of the perceived difficulties:* From my readings of hundreds of pupil files I have no doubt that some pupil difficulties are frequently spoken of by the staff of a school between themselves, and are so taken for granted that clear, unambiguous, but sympathetically put information is not given to parents. Indeed I have seen written reports in which the blandness or fear of talking straight positively obscure the truth. For instance, a junior school leaving report on a particularly disturbed boy, whose bi-lingual African parents had only recently come to this country, and whose English was limited, had: 'He is impervious to normal sanctions' as the only description of his disruptive behaviour. Bombshells of bad news lead to rejection of referral. *Successful referral requires previous discussion of the difficulties.*

(c) *School knowledge of the agency*
Referral can feel like (and indeed sometimes is) rejection by the school community and ejection to some unknown and distant person or institution. It often implies that the school, in which parents have put their trust, is severing all future connection. I have noticed over the years that when my GP 'refers' me or a member of my family to a specialist he almost always indicates his personal knowledge of that specialist. I have also noticed that parents are far happier to consider a referral if I know personally the individual to whom the suggested referral is to be made or if I know the head of the institution: 'I'm sure my friend Mrs. X, whom I admire, will consider your case carefully' is professionally better than 'You can try the X institution. They can probably help'! *Successful referral requires personal inter-professional knowledge.*

(d) *Accompanied visits*
   Even if a school has met the three conditions I have outlined in a, b, and c, the initial visit to the other agency may be so daunting as to be totally disabling. Teachers need to be able to imagine what it is like to take your child (and yourself!) to a psycho-therapist. There are some occasions on which I should recommend the family are accompanied by an appropriate member of the school's staff. *Successful referral requires confidence in and familiarity with the person or institution to which the family are being referred.*

Home Visiting

In the establishment of a central school/home partnership in search of a child's welfare mutual understanding and trust are essential. But also there has to be mutual support — one partner sometimes and at others the other suggesting, wondering, asking for advice, reminding, urging. In many cases this partnership can be established by the visit of parents or guardians to school, by post, and by phone. Indeed a relaxed use of the phone can be very valuable as it allows brief but personal interchange unhampered by the environment. (Interestingly some school brochures in Denmark and the Netherlands give home phone numbers of teachers [Macbeth, 1984, p. 47].)

However, there are some home/school relationships and some occasions in a larger number for which a visit to the pupil's home is immensely and uniquely valuable. When the focus is directly, completely, and solely on the *welfare* of the pupil, a discussion in her or his home has the following advantages:

(i)   The school's representative has demonstrated sufficient concern to visit, and this fact alone is encouraging to parents or guardians;
(ii) the pupil's parents or guardians are on *their* home ground, offering *their* hospitality, and this often gives them an added confidence and willingness to share;
(iii) in the home, the centrality of the pupil is symbolically more obvious and powerful than in school, where convenience for the school's systems can loom larger.
(iv) only in the pupil's own home setting is it possible to really learn about her or his background sympathetically, and to learn from parents or guardians.

Of course, home visits take longer per pupil than a neatly organized sequence of parent visitors by appointment at school. This time point *is* important, for in a heavily packed professional life time lost is time taken from another pupil. I nevertheless recommend a regular cycle of home visits. In these sessions questions about the pupil's welfare needs can be explored with a sympathy and honesty that is not always possible in school. Out of these explorations can come agreed strategies for action, contracted programmes, and joint approaches to more specialized services. Home visiting is not a 'cure all' to be used lavishly or over-hopefully, but it is a potentially powerful act in the school's repertoire for improving the welfare of children.

Time

Where could the professional time for this contact come from? In the 'practical' questions facing education authorities and schools which Alastair Macbeth isolates (Macbeth, 1984, p. 182) he includes: 'Many teachers have become accustomed to an occupational routine which does *not* include regular contact with families/parents'. This is certainly so, and can be changed only by a combination of approaches, including his 'implications for teachers' terms of service and pay'. A nation cannot ask too much of any group of its professional servants.

It is difficult to see how the flexible requirements of good liaison could be met by some of the proposals made to provide the capacity in the profession for it. For instance, Macbeth quotes 'liaison pay' (special payments for liaison overtime) and 'status opting' (whereby certain teachers with full professional status and higher pay take on the open-ended commitment, but others are contractually less flexible 'day teachers') (Macbeth, 1984, p. 191). The former would give liaison a different status from any other of the profession's tasks, and would make its motives suspect. The latter would not fit the 'one profession' concept that UK teachers and their unions value so highly.

In the English and Welsh school at least, the prime leadership task for home links is that of the 'pastoral staff' (see Marland, 1974). As long ago as 1963, the Newsom report argued:

> There may be a strong case for having additional members of staff who have special responsibilities for home visiting, and who act as liaison officers with all the other medical, welfare,

and child care services in the district. (Central Advisory Council, 1963, p. 70)

I fear that this could lead to a separating of functions. On the other hand, a school could have such specialists, who could be called on to supplement others when necessary. This could be particularly valuable for, for instance, liaison with certain ethnic minority groups, for whom special language and cultural knowledge is important.

I should argue strongly against 'specialist home-school liaison teachers' being the general rule (Macbeth, *op cit*), for a number of reasons, chiefly that on the one hand parents will not so fully accept this mode of communication, and on the other hand that the valuable learning about the families will not thus be generalized throughout the staff.

I can suggest only that a study is made of the precise time implications of all those exhortations in government-sponsored reports. Perhaps a pilot plan should be introduced in one area, and evaluated. Then the hours required could be roughly estimated. In my view these would best be met by an ear-marked addition to teaching staff resources with obligations (however they are dispersed) to devote the agreed time to liaison.

Facilities

Good home/school links for pupils' welfare, it regrettably has to be pointed out, depend also on the mechanics of communication: reception facilities, telephones, typing. Most UK schools are lamentably under-provided, and no one appears to have troubled to have translated the concept of 'keeping in touch with homes' into practical outlines of the consequential facilities required. Dictating and audio-typing facilities for pastoral team leaders would do more good than continued rhetoric and exhortation!

Conclusions

The welfare needs of *all* pupils required the 'generalist' parent or guardian and the 'generalist' school teacher to know each other well, respect each other's stance, and, above all, be able to work effectively together as partners. Each needs to understand and respect the *differences*, and thus, paradoxically, be the more able to collaborate.

Each LEA and within that each school needs a coherent (family liaison policy which will encourage and facilitate mutually complementary home/school liaison procedures to enhance the welfare of pupils.

Learning from Parents

At the end of their study of young children learning in the nursery school and at home, Barbara Tizard and Martin Hughes were driven to the conclusion which could stand as an epigraph to schools' welfare work with parents and their children:

> It is time to shift the emphasis away from what parents should learn from professionals, and towards what professionals can learn from studying parents and children at home. (Tizard and Hughes, 1984, p. 267)

This learning will help schools judge more appropriately. There will be times when the overall welfare of a pupil will be judged best served by disagreeing with parents, by over-ruling them, even sometimes by recommending that social services consider a care order. More often, though, the need is to help parents with *their* wishes to support the welfare of their child.

'Good home/school relations' are now axiomatically 'a good thing' and most heads would claim their school's 'home/school relations' as 'second to none'! However, it is not always clear what is being referred to. The Mortimores put it clearly in their study of early childhood education:

> Discussion of home school relations is made difficult by a lack of a common definition of the term 'parent involvement'. To some, the term means the active presence of parents within the school (helping in the classroom, making and mending equipment); to others, it implies that parents are involved in the management and decision-making processes of the school; yet others understand little more than parents being energetic and generous in raising funds for the school, conscientious in their attendance at social events, and friendly in their relations with staff. (Mortimore, J. and P., 1984, p. 1)

There is, though, a fourth definition that does not exclude those activities but does not logically require them, that is a professional/lay working relationship designed *to complement and facilitate what members of the family can themselves do*: 'We had the impression of a widespread resourcefulness amongst parents, even parents who were not themselves highly educated.' (Johnson and Ransom, 1983, p. 95) It is that resourcefulness that the school should amplify and complement in working with parents for the welfare of the young people.

Pastoral Care for Children: Welfare for Teachers

Robert Laslett
University of Birmingham

I am prompted to write this chapter by consideration of the argument that Derek Williamson advances in his illuminating chapter 'Pastoral care or "Pastoralization"' in Best, Jarvis and Ribbins (1980) *Perspectives on Pastoral Care*. I believe that Williamson has identified and described important aspects of the ways in which pastoral care systems operate in schools, but that he does not extend his argument far enough. I think that his analysis of pastoral care might be extended to consider teachers' needs, and that their needs can be legitimately considered in relation to welfare provisions for staff. By welfare I mean 'The state or condition of doing or being well ... happiness or well being (of a person, community or thing); thriving, successful, progress in life ...' (*Oxford English Dictionary*). I am not concerned with all aspects of school life which affect teachers' effectiveness, such as environment or conditions of service. I am concentrating on their need for welfare in relation to their teaching. I wish to emphasize the point that considerations of the welfare of teachers cannot be separated from considerations of the good of the child as a pupil.

In his chapter Williamson points out that pastoral care systems are designed to assist schools in two ways. Class tutors concerned with pastoral care establish what he calls 'a relationship of mutual trust' between themselves and children in their tutorial groups. For children who show that they are able to make good use of the learning opportunities the school offers, tutors make use of this relationship to advise them on the ways that they can make best use of these. But the tutors also make use of their relationship of mutual trust to influence those whose performance indicates that the school does not provide appropriate learning opportunities. In this they '. . . knowingly or otherwise deflect the legitimate grievance (of these children) away from the inadequate learning experiences offered within the system . . .' They are fortified in this by the readiness with which they impute faults or weaknesses to the child, implying that these are within him. They accept the 'disability perspective' readily, which places responsibility for failure on the child without due reference to the limitations of the educational environment.

In this way, unsuccessful children meet the negative aspect of pastoral care. In Williamson's term, they are 'pastoralized.' This process of pastoralization then serves two purposes. It assists teachers in their justification that unsuccessful children, especially those whose behaviour causes concern, need activities and experiences designed to increase their socialization. Without it, these children in schools which emphasize 'product teaching' (education approached as the production of a standardized commodity) might act out their resentment and frustrations. Pastoralization also serves to disguise the consequences of 'inadequate teaching methods'. He suggests that if teachers were more competent, there would be no need for pastoralization, and pastoral care systems would be freed to be of service to children whose difficulties do not stem from inadequacies of the school system. Class tutors could then give their attention to more legitimate demands, making better use of their relationships with children and the mutual trust that characterizes these. As pastoral care systems operate at present, children cannot challenge the school's inadequate teaching methods. Tutors do not explore the inadequacies of the school's provision as a cause of children's difficulties or an aggravation of them. Tutors soften up the unsuccessful children to accept what the school provides, bolstering up their prescription with demonstrating or implying that the children's lack of success is due to their own inadequacies. Successful pastoralization persuades children to accept this view of themselves.

Williamson argues that improvements in curriculum will improve pastoral care systems: '. . . I shall argue that problems which pastoral care systems supposedly exist to solve, may perhaps be solved by a much wider consideration of the nature and processes of teaching and learning' (p. 172). But attention to the curriculum is not enough. What is also needed is more attention to the welfare of the teachers who plan and implement the curriculum.

Thus Williamson identifies and describes a paradoxical situation. The success of pastoralization is really a failure in pastoral care. But when he points to inadequate teaching methods as being the ground from which pastoralization springs, he does not explore the probability that these methods are frequently the consequence of another failure in care — the absence or inadequacy of welfare extended to teachers.

Constraints Upon Teachers' Asking for Help

One of the difficulties teachers have, especially those with little experience of working in secondary schools, is the expectation of their colleagues and the children that they will always be successful despite the wide variety of demands made upon them. For teachers who find that this expectation is too high, they have another problem which the conventions of many schools emphasize — that if they seek help when in difficulties they are admitting to professional failure. This was brought home by the account of a teacher, potentially a very effective one — who was having problems with a class with some notorious disrupters in it. When she reached the staffroom at break time, she said in answer to a question about her obvious distress, that she had just had 'an awful time with 4K.' At this a senior member of staff said, '4K? They never give me a moment's trouble!' This reduced the unfortunate teacher to tears.

Now it is not unreasonable to expect teachers who have had some years of professional training, to do their job properly. And many do. All schools seem to have on the staff teachers with an invincible air of authority who are imperturbable and unfailingly effective. Sometimes such teachers are said to have a great deal of charisma, or that they are 'naturals'. I believe that there are such teachers, although charisma does not altogether explain their success, if this is regarded as some magical quality. Close observation of charismatic teachers shows that apart from gifts of personality, they deploy skills which they have learned. The fact that charisma is not enough is demonstrated in the wealth of the publications which describe the processes of effective classroom management. But there are also many schools where the staff recognize that some colleague or colleagues have considerable difficulties in classrooms. This is sometimes acknowledged in staff rooms by comments such as 'We have to carry old Jones.' This is usually said in rather hushed tones which illustrates that teachers consider that it is not quite the thing to suggest criticism of a colleague whose need for help is seen to be a weakness, as if old Jones was not very intelligent or was suffering from a malignant illness.

Teachers' failures in classrooms are public failures. Teachers are acutely aware that when they fail, their failures are observed and commented on by children. As if this were not unpleasant enough, some teachers who fail in front of their classes, strive to prevent colleagues from knowing about it, because they believe that failure, even in difficult circumstances, reflects on their professional competence. Many teachers would save themselves much distress if they could get away from the notion that to admit to being vulnerable does not imply admission of incompetence. Their anxiety associated with public failure and the perception that they had better keep this quiet is compounded by their feelings of disappointment and frustration with themselves. This inevitably increases their stress. This, in turn, increases the probability that their performance will deteriorate.

The Teacher's Hook

It is true that recognition of the difficulties that many teachers encounter in classrooms has led to the provision of programmes of in-service training in schools and in-service courses organised by local education authorities. But this is not so in all schools or in all authorities, and even where such courses are available, there is another difficulty. Some teachers whose teaching methods are inadequate do not recognize this and do not recognize their need to improve. They have devised their methods and as these are effective with the majority of children, they persist with them. For those children whom they consider atypical, they have a solution to offer, and in some circumstances, to insist upon. The children need some additional provision if the discrepancy between their performance and the expected standard is not very marked. If it is very marked, then they need some form of special educational provision. For some where the discrepancy suggests that they need some extra provision, then pastoral care is indicated. In this sense the teacher gets off the hook. They are impaled upon it by their unwillingness or their inability to adapt their teaching methods so that they provide appropriate learning for all the children in their classes. In getting off the hook by their use of pastoral care, they do not perceive that they are taking a negative stance towards children — and in Williamson's view, a considerable number of children.

Williamson recognizes that this use of the pastoral care system — pastoralization — is a means of relieving the system, of persuading the child that he is at fault because he cannot meet its demands.

Ineffectual teaching methods are not called into question. But there remains the problem of persuading the teacher that he needs help to provide appropriate learning opportunities for all the children in the class, and considering how this help might be provided.

Thus we can see that teachers' need of help and the difficulties associated with seeking it, are very real. There is the teacher who is obviously in difficulties but who feels that admission of these is an admission of professional failure. These feelings inhibit or prevent her from seeking assistance. Unless her difficulties are so acute that she either breaks down, or at the point of breakdown the truth of her situation forces others to come to her assistance, then it is quite likely that she will adopt and persist in methods which are, in fact, inadequate but which she adopts for her own survival. At the point when she adopts her survival procedures, if she were confident that she could discuss whatever problems she meets with a supportive figure on the staff, two advantages would follow. She would relieve her anxieties, and she could be helped to devise her own methods of teaching appropriate for the unsuccessful children. At this point she is an easier person to help than the teacher who has settled for a conservative mode. The intervention, which would involve recognition of teachers' needs and providing appropriate support, seems to be lacking. One way in which this may be supplied is through the activities of a supportive teacher, which will be considered later in the chapter.

Teachers' Needs In Training and In Practice

When discussing initial training programmes with teachers, it seems that there are important matters which are treated too superficially, or are overlooked. Among these are strategies for avoiding stress or reducing unavoidable stress, more understanding of the strength of the feelings in children that are directed at teachers, knowledge of the dynamics that operate in groups of children, and the management of children who either resist or defy teachers. Ignorance of these, and of opportunities to practise skills under supervision, increases the probability that potentially effective teachers will adopt classroom strategies that appear as inadequate teaching methods.

Those concerned with initial training of teachers have a great deal to do to prepare students for teaching, and, with reference to the topics mentioned, they do have real difficulties. They cannot prepare students for all the situations they will meet in schools. They cannot replicate situations which prepare students for the responsibilities, and the isolation, which teachers meet when they are on their own in charge of classes. Many aspects of a teacher's task can only be learned from experience of teaching. The question that arises is, experience of doing what? If it is experience of teaching in a system that has the disadvantages that Williamson has described, then this reduces the probability that schools will reach the expectations that they will provide appropriate education for all the children in them. This accountability is now more likely to be demanded than before, and it is accountability with a new element. The provision of appropriate learning has to include a larger proportion of children with special needs. This only emphasizes the need of supports for teachers if they are to be as innovative and imaginative as the future requires.

Teacher Stress

One of the most important tasks that could be asked of anyone concerned with teachers' welfare would be to help teachers manage the stress that arises from teaching. Although not all teachers find this stress a problem, many do, as Dunham (1976, 1981, 1984) Kyriacou and Sutcliffe (1977, 1979, 1978) and Kyriacou (1980) have demonstrated. In an interesting study, Kyriacou asked teachers from two comprehensive schools to rank frequency of use of strategies for the reduction of stress. Their list includes some effective strategies, but two features of their ranking are worth looking at. The first is that some of the strategies the teachers propose suggest that they have not had much help to increase their understanding of stress as an important factor which affects their classroom performance. Their proposals, for example, that stress can be reduced by assuring themselves that everything will be all right, or that teachers who worry about events in the classroom should try not to worry, are rather naive. Again, although the suggested strategy that to forget work when the day is done is sound for many, it is not likely to help those who do not have much evidence that stressful events will not recur. The most frequently chosen strategy — 'Try to keep things in perspective' — is just what teachers under stress find very difficult to do unless someone helps them to draw out the perspective. One of the features of high anxiety and stress is that it narrows perceptions (Dohrenwend, 1961). Those under stress do not perceive the alternatives that are available. Another person who is aware, or made aware, of a stressful situation does not have to *invent* all these alternatives.

They are in the situation itself, but stress prevents their appreciation. Listening to teachers describe situations which cause them undue anxiety, we hear phrases like, 'Now I see what I could have done,' or 'Why didn't I notice that at the time?', 'Why didn't I think of that?'

Another interesting feature of the teachers' ranking of effective strategies for reducing stress is the lowest ranking of two of them. These are; 'Talk about the situation with someone else at work,'and, 'Express your irritation to colleagues at work and let off steam.' Since talking to another person and expressing feelings of irritation and frustration are recognized as being very effective in reducing stress, it is surprising to see these so low in the ranking. It suggests that these teachers at least — and very probably many others — do not have opportunities to find a sympathetic listener.

Smith (1982) has described how teachers can 'help colleagues cope.' The member of staff who does this has a sensitive task, but it can be done, as Smith illustrates. It is worth while emphasizing that it can be done, not by a 'steam cabin therapist', as Redl and Wineman (1951, 1952) describe a very skilled and high powered counsellor, but by a teacher's colleague. It is important to underline that point because welfare for teachers does not mean that money has to be found to pay extra staff from outside the school. Teachers can help themselves if they understand what seeking help and providing it involves. Certainly this implies a willingness to change in those who seek help, and it also implies that teachers understand themselves as well as understanding their tasks. Indeed, teachers' self understanding helps them to understand their tasks better and to teach children more effectively.

Teachers' Need for Self Understanding

One of the most potent sources of stress for teachers is the presence of poorly motivated and disruptive children in their classes, but it is not this minority of children and the problems they cause to teachers that I want to consider now, although teachers' reactions to them cannot be separated from Williamson's contention about the negative uses of the pastoral care system. If the curriculum is threadbare, if there is no common agreement among the staff about behavioural management, those children who are most aware of these deficiences or most resentful of the school's inadequate responses to their needs, are more likely to be disruptive than those who can succeed with the educational fare that is offered. A teacher who finds that his repertoire of management skills or teaching skills are not sufficient, may not be able to face the stress of working with these children or adapting his teaching to reduce their resentment. He has to get off the hook and make use of the pastoral care system in the ways that Williamson describes.

It is tempting to put down teachers' poor performance to their incompetence. There are incompetent teachers, as there are incompetent doctors, civil servants and parsons. But behind many displays of incompetence in teachers there is high anxiety. How teachers recognise the effects of their high anxiety, how they cope with it so that it does not unsettle children and add to their own difficulties, is another feature of training courses which does not receive enough attention. For teacher anxiety effects children and their performance. The teachers who are unduly anxious demonstrate this in the classrooms by the way that they organize or disorganize lessons. Their anxiety shows in the way they talk, the way they move, by their jumpy behaviour and their obvious unease. One of the most impressive characteristics of an effective teacher is the children's perception of her as someone who is in control, not only of them, but of herself. Such a teacher gives the clue to her equanimity by the self control which is discernible even in the minutiae of her actual behaviour, which cues the children into the behaviour she wants. The highly anxious teacher gives cues to the kind of behaviour she does not want, and probably cannot manage.

If we consider the often repeated phrase that teachers use about children in school — 'We are in loco parentis' — then this helps to illuminate an aspect of teachers' tasks which has implications which they sometimes overlook. If they are in loco parentis, this does not only mean they are responsible for children whom they prevent from behaviours that their parents would not allow and which they assume teachers will not permit. This is a negative construction of the phrase. There is also the positive construction of this phrase. Children perceive teachers as having a parental role. This is usually more noticeable in primary schools than in secondary schools and primary school teachers accept it readily. For many of them it is an attractive feature of their work. Now, as it is true that teachers, without seeking it, assume a parenting role, then this leads into consideration of the feelings that children direct towards their parents. On the whole, those children who most nearly fit the teachers' idea of the ideal pupil have good relationships with their parents. Thus their relationships with their teachers are positive. They accept the stress of learning, frustration, competition, criticism, or punishment and the sharing of the teacher with other children. These fortunate children have internalized a good image of parental affection, authority and concern. They have also had countless opportunities to learn appropriate behaviour from good models whom they wish to emulate and please. When they displace their feelings towards their parents on to the teacher, these are good feelings.

No classes contain *only* such children. Teachers are the recipients of a variety of feelings that children have towards their parents. Included among this variety are feelings of resentment at parental behaviour, resentment at parental expressions of negative feelings towards them. Depending upon the child-parent relationship, there are likely to be children in any class who are jealous of their parents, envious of them, hostile towards them, indifferent towards them. When these children displace these feelings on to teachers, they displace bad feelings. When they project on to the teacher their own shortcomings or weaknesses, they project negative feelings about themselves. Their behaviour seems inexplicable to teachers, who frequently comment that it is. They are surprised and dismayed by the reaction of a child, who, for example, reacts to a reasonable request or reasonable criticism, with hostility. What the teachers overlook is that the same mechanism may be at work then as when a child co-operates with a smile. But the sequel to the hostility is very different, although this does depend upon the teacher concerned, the place and the audience.

Thus teachers need to be more aware of their situation as targets for a wide range of feelings, some of them being very strong feelings. They recognize that they are the focal point in lessons to which children's attentions are directed. What they overlook is that they are also a focal point for children's feelings, some of them being transferred feelings. Teachers have sometimes to demand children's attention; children's feelings about their teachers are spontaneous. When teachers understand this they also understand, and are therefore more likely to reduce or prevent, inexplicable negative behaviours which have their origin in feelings in situations which the teacher cannot control.

But as Wittenberg and her co-authors make clear (Wittenberg *et al.* 1983), being aware of children's feelings and responding to them from a basis of understanding, is not all the awareness of feelings that teachers need. They also need to be as aware as possible of their own feelings as these are elicited by children's behaviour, or the verbal expression of their feelings. An emotional encounter with a child — hearing their spiteful or affectionate comment, being the recipient of hostile or seductive feelings — sets up reverberations in teachers. They have to deal with these feelings. They may be kindly or affectionate feelings or hostile and angry ones, but whatever they are, teachers have to take care how they act them out. Kindly feelings can lead on to showing favouritism or possessiveness or jealousy. A teacher who feels very positively towards a child may not be aware of the stealthy way these feelings grow, although other children who do not share his feelings for the child are aware of it because they see favouritism. When these warm feelings towards a child reduce the professional distance that teachers need to preserve — the distance need not be very long or icy — then their interactions with the child are hampered by their feelings. As most teachers describe this, their colleague is too involved with a child and has lost his objectivity. If this continues, a difficult situation arises. The teacher needs the child's good feelings and preserves these by making undue allowances for him, or giving him more credit than is due. Whatever form this expression of too warm feelings take, they interfere with a teacher's impartiality. Teachers do depend upon their positive relationships with children to teach them successfully, but they must not have dependent feelings towards any of them. This would be confusing for the child concerned, other children and colleagues. It would be a role reversal, because children depend upon their teachers. While it is true that teachers have professional conventions to guide them in their relationships with children, these cannot prevent feelings from arising, nor do they always regulate teachers' behaviour.

This is often more plainly seen if a child arouses very strong negative feelings in a teacher. This teacher then has a problem. How does she deal with her feelings about the child, who may have aroused her strong dislike, her anger or hostility? Her anger, for example, has to go somewhere. If it goes out then it will alight on a child, and not always the one who has aroused the anger, with consequences she did not intend and could not foresee. If the anger goes in then the teacher still has some problems with it, although she is then in a better position to deal with it than when it was first aroused. After the crisis has passed, the child who has not her maturity and control is at least spared from its immediate effects.

It is not true that it is inappropriate for teachers to show anger. They are human beings, and human beings are likely to be angry if they are continually provoked or frustrated or humiliated in the presence of those whom they are expected to manage and instruct. Furthermore, children understand expressions of anger and they appreciate them. What they cannot manage is teachers' uncontrolled, unpredictable or intemperate anger, because this is either frightening or ridiculous. How children perceive it depends upon the resilience of their personalities and on their experiences of intemperately angry people. If a teacher is angry too frequently, then this suggests that something or some things are going wrong which should be looked at, but very effective and well liked teachers show their anger at times. Some teachers suggest that it is appropriate to simulate anger, but there seems no need to do this. It seems best either to be angry or not. It is a pity to devalue a genuine feeling. What is important is that teachers are aware that they have angry feelings and that some children or some child will breach their defences and they will show their anger. It is as much a genuine bit of them as their benevolence or affection, and knowing this about themselves prevents them from being surprised at their angry feelings and from feeling undue guilt about the expression of them with as much control as they can manage. The fact that teachers do feel guilty about their anger, and sorry that it got the better of them at times, is illustrated by their conversations in staff rooms, and also by their comments in class-rooms to children who witnessed their anger.

These considerations apply to other feelings of course. Although it sounds unprofessional for teachers to talk in these terms, there are some children who stir up real hostility in some teachers. There can be no other explanation of some of the unpleasant things that some teachers either say or do to some children, and common experience of schools shows that this happens. In this connection it is interesting to remember what a very skilled and perceptive psycho-analyst and paediatrician once admitted. Although it is not easy to envisage the scene, apparently one child so exasperated or so wounded Winnicott that he put him outside his consulting room. He writes. 'Did I hit him? No, I did not hit, but I may have done had I not known all about my hate....' (Winnicott 1958).

These are negative feelings, but there are positive feelings aroused in teachers as well. They are pleasant, and do not lead on to guilty feelings or the same kind of conflicts that accompany the negative feelings because they accord with teachers' perceptions of their role and the expectations of others about their role. But they need recognition and managing as the negative feelings do. Many problems arise because of unadmitted and unrecognized feelings of jealousy and possessiveness towards children who are attractive to teachers.

There are other aspects of the reverberation to which Wittenberg has drawn attention. Teachers cannot escape from the memories of their own childhood experiences, nor from interactions with children which are likely to remind them of these. If these memories are good ones, then they can resolve emotional encounters with children happily with reference to their own experiences. This is an advantage to them as it is of direct assistance in discharge of the parenting role involved in teaching. But there can be no guarantee that teachers, as with any other sections of the population, were uniformly fortunate in their childhoods, however successfully they have accommodated any negative feelings associated with earlier experiences. Thus in some emotional encounters with a child or some children, what the children say or do, not only to them but to other children, may be too reminiscent of those childhood situations which caused them pain. The behaviour may also remind them of their own vulnerabilities which they have overcome at some cost and the recollection of these vulnerabilities and the cost of endeavours to overcome them, all forced into their consciousness by the behaviour they witness, increases the stress of meeting emotional demands made upon them.

This consideration of teachers' awareness of their own feelings may suggest that their success in meeting the emotional discharges in classrooms must involve counselling at levels which are not only inappropriate but impossible. But this is not so. The welfare envisaged for teachers would involve a colleague who would remind teachers of the reality of the strength of the feelings directed towards them in classrooms, that their own feelings are engaged, and that their irritation, or anger, or hostility, as well as their affection, are legitimate feelings but that they have to be aware of their effects. The colleague would have to remind them that it is not much use relying on professionalism as if this would provide immunity. Their professional tasks bring them into contact with feelings and their own responses to these sometimes causes stress. The colleague would allow teachers to open up topics which seem to be kept too much out of the way in schools.

It is now common practice in residential social work to have a 'key worker' who co-ordinates the activities of all those who have responsibilities for the child, and to whom the child turns for advice on issues which affect her. In America there is the 'master teacher' whose skills and knowledge enable her to teach effectively in a variety of situations which are beyond the scope of less well trained and less experienced colleagues. Welfare for teachers could be provided by a similar figure — the 'support teacher' who shows that he has developed skills in listening and prompting colleagues to talk freely about their stress and difficulties. If he has managed to acquire counselling skills, then this is a decided advantage, but it need not be a prerequisite for the task. Some teachers are able, almost by the light of nature, to convey to colleagues their awareness of their problems and their sensitivity and sense. They are busy people of course, but a school staff determined to find some solution to the problems of stress among their colleagues, could manage to overcome this problem of time away from the classroom for the key teacher. It is too important to leave to chance.

The support teacher's primary task would be to help colleagues to reduce stress. But this does not imply that he would assist in camouflaging the shortcomings of an inadequate system, but rather the opposite. He would assist in reducing those stresses which teachers would find in a more demanding and more appropriate system.

Sources of Stress in Classrooms

A very potent cause of stress to teachers is the management of disruptive pupils in classrooms. It is difficult to be precise about the extent of disruptive behaviour, because there are difficulties in determining this satisfactorily. Laslett (1977) has reviewed studies of the prevalence of disruptive and violent behaviour in schools and has summarized the difficulties of collecting data. Another source of information is the media, but these are not reliable sources because of the noticeable tendency for them to exaggerate incidents of violent and disruptive behaviour for their news value. This was clearly demonstrated by a television programme in the early seventies which showed the difficulties some teachers encountered in a London comprehensive school. The staff at the school were most indignant that the programme producer omitted to point out that they showed disruptive incidents taking place in probationary teachers' classes and did not include scenes with the same pupils working satisfactorily with more experienced teachers.

Nevertheless, it is true that teachers in many schools now have to manage children who more frequently resist their authority and present them with difficult problems of control. It is also true that teachers complain that in their initial training not enough attention was given to teaching them skills of classroom management, and there are schools where there is no well organized and commonly agreed approach to discipline (Rutter *et al.* 1979), and where the school curriculum is not appropriate. But these factors alone do not explain the problem. Teachers have not become dramatically less efficient during the last ten years. The education service, although not magnanimously funded, is not decrepit.

There have been significant alterations in attitudes to authority during the last twenty years, there is more actual violence in our society which is portrayed on television and reported in the press. There is more fictional violence and aggressive behaviour constantly available to children. There are changes in the patterns of parental authority, and a change in the status of adolescents among whom teachers find the sharpest challenges to their authority.

It is easy to overlook that among the young hooligans who cause havoc on the football ground terraces on Saturdays, and have little compunction in challenging the police and defying adults are those who are in classrooms on Monday mornings. Apart from the problems of managing their behaviour, teachers are conscious that the disaffected pupils are aware that their futures are not very alluring. It is improbable that changes that affect the adolescent's prospects of employment — independence — security according to the pattern common to their parents and grandparents, does not affect their self perceptions, their perceptions of their schools and the way they behave. Furthermore, while in school they are expected to do as they are told, outside school they are encouraged, by very powerful interests, to do as they wish. Because adolescents now have a larger share of the family income than their parents had, they are a section of the population with money to spend, and targets for those who persuade and cajole them to spend it on their products. In school they are relatively powerless, outside schools they have power. This is another aspect of the change in the relative status of teachers and pupils. It is complicated by the fact that the pupils' status is not a settled one because of the emotional, physical and psychological changes during adolescence. The extensive literature devoted to classroom management (Brophy and Evertson 1976, Kounin 1970, Lemlech 1979, Marland 1975, Robertson 1980, Laslett and Smith 1984) and the number of in-service courses which focus on this topic show that it is a matter of prime concern to teachers, and difficulties in management are sources of stress. This raises two questions; how well were teachers trained in the techniques of classroom management, and how well are they supported when they find this difficult in schools?

The answer to the first question is not very reassuring. From talking to teachers about their initial training, it seems that their tutors hardly liked to suggest that awkward and very testing incidents would arise in well planned and imaginatively presented lessons. This cannot be discounted, but it does not take into account the factors influencing pupils' attitudes to authority mentioned earlier. There are some awkward customers in many schools whose behaviour is very different from their behaviour and their tutors' behaviour when they were at school. In particular, initial training courses seem to overlook preparation of teachers in these particulars.

(a) *Knowledge of the processes at work in small groups with a leader*, which classes of children closely resemble. Among the processes that teachers should be aware of are; the use by a class of a child who represents, or acts out, the resentment or hostility of the whole class; the class use of the licensed wag or the licensed challenger to teachers' authority; the class use of a scapegoat; the projection on to the teacher of class feeling of inadequacy; the reality of what Redl and Wineman (1951, 1952) have described as 'psychological suction' (when children who usually behave appropriately are unable to resist the temptations of exciting and forbidden events)

(b) *Knowledge of the importance of non verbal communications*. Many teachers seem to be unaware of the effects of their posture, gait, gesture and demeanour. Body language is strong language, and whereas teachers recognize that challenging comments may lead to a confrontation, they quite overlook the challenge they present to children bold enough to rise to it, by the way they point, scowl, or move. Robertson (1980) has shown that a teacher's faltering stance, her use of her own space in the classroom, and her perception of children's space, all affect her management.

(c) *Knowledge of ways of avoiding useless confrontations with children*, and how to manage those that are unavoidable. It is quite extraordinary to observe how some teachers blunder into confrontations which they do not wish for and cannot manage, and which have no positive outcome. There are times when confrontation is appropriate, but there are skills in the management of these which need to be known. There are also skills of disengagement from confrontations wished upon teachers by children who relish them, and these disengagement skills need to be known.

Conclusion

While there is evidence that initial training of teachers might equip them better for some of the classroom events which await them, we cannot overlook the fact that it is only when these events unfold that teachers realise that they need help. They can increase their skills by attending in-service courses, but they need more immediate help when taken unawares by some disaster which raises their anxiety and feelings of frustration and disappointment with themselves. It is then that some form of welfare is needed. If schools are to provide appropriate learning for all the children in them, then teachers have a right to believe that the education service should value them as its most important asset. Part of this valuing is provision of appropriate training for a demanding task. Another is demonstrating care for their welfare. This is not only good of itself. It is necessary to prevent potentially effective teachers from adopting inadequate teaching methods. Without it there is a poor return on the capital invested in their training. This has a direct bearing on the issues that Williamson raises in his descriptions of the negative uses of pastoral care and the convenience of pastoralization.

Concepts of Welfare and Ability in Remedial Education

Ron Best
Chelmer Institute of Higher Education

When I was in the fifth and final year of the (Australian) comprehensive school I attended, some of our lessons — Economics I fancy — were held in a room which overlooked the open-air basket-ball courts. These were, in fact, areas of sun-baked clay with rudimentary side-lines scratched into the dirt with a stick, and recognizable for what they were only by virtue of the posts with their rings and back-boards at each end. I recall one morning having the lesson interrupted by a loud and singularly tuneless whistling. Everyone turned to the window. There, perched on a ladder with his slim body through the 'basket', was a young lad totally engrossed in covering the back-board with a thick and dripping coat of white paint. He was one of the 'GA's' — 'General Activities', one label for the remedial children of that time and place — and with the natural superiority of the academic successes that we were, we all laughed at this spectacle. 'There's a man happy in his work', observed the teacher, dragging our attention back to the mysteries of the kinked Demand-curve.

In a way, the problematics of the whole area of remedial education are encapsulated in this memory. What that lad was doing was useful and, it seems, fulfilling: whether that was true of what we were doing is less certain. Yet his experience was to count as nothing compared to the certificates we would have when we left school. The rest of his curriculum literacy, numeracy and a watered-down academic experience best described as 'General Knowledge' — would have aimed to bring him up to some minimum standard in 'the basics' such that he would at least be able to 'get by in life' without looking too foolish too often. Yet he would always be separated from his 'betters' even in the 'classless society', by the gulf between the professions and the manual workers, between the 'educated' and the 'uneducated', between the 'educational successes' and the 'educational failures'.

The roles of the teachers in that school were also indicative. Our teachers were, first and foremost, teachers of subjects, academics whom we respected for their mastery of a discipline and whom we liked in rough proportion to their ability to make a lesson enjoyable if often by means quite extrinsic to their avowed purpose. *His* teachers would have been non-graduates, often 'up-graded' from years of teaching in primary schools, and more than likely sentenced to spend most of their time-table in a demountable, insulated from the rest of the school by a space of symbolic significance greater than any geographical distance could convey. Yet such teachers often displayed a dedication and warmth which we 'successes' would have welcomed in some of our own teachers, and, it has to be said, a possessive protectiveness which seemed in our eyes, to add to the 'separateness' and 'oddness' of their flock. Their commitment to the *welfare* of their children was never in question, but like welfare services in general, an unhealthy paternalism and the stigmatizing of the beneficiaries were amongst the unintended consequences of their good intentions.

In this chapter, I want to raise these issues afresh, in an empirical comment from an on-going investigation of the organization of remedial provision in two comprehensive schools.

If there is a 'conventional wisdom' of remedial education, it is a conventional wisdom rooted in a particular concept of education and educability, a concept which is predominantly to do with the cognitive development of the individual in the context of a world of comparisons. Dominated by psychology — and especially the influential work of Burt, Vernon and others concerned with measurement — the 'theory and practice' of remedial provision has been premised upon a set of basic assumptions which are susceptible to more or less criticism. One assumption is that ability or 'intelligence' is some innate, inherited, and 'fixed' cognitive ability — a finite reservoir of capacity to 'work things out', if you like — which is either more or less fully utilized but whose volume cannot be altered. A second assumption is that this ability is distributed throughout the population according to the requirements of a bell-shaped graph known as the 'curve of normal distribution', that most people have a quota of this ability somewhere around the average for the population, while a lesser number are to be found with 'gifts' towards each of the extremes. In the curious absurdity of conventional thinking, only children whose IQ scores are around the mean in this distribution are thought of as being 'normal': those at or near the extremes are in some way abnormal – either as the 'gifted' or as the 'subnormal'. The latter idea is enshrined in formal educational categories of the ESN(M) and ESN(S) children who, to date, have been most often separately catered for in special schools of one sort or another. Somewhere between the 'normal' child and the extreme, is one instance of the 'remedial child': the child of low intelligence but not sufficiently so to warrant education in a special institution.

In a way it is curious for the word 'remedial' to be applied to such children at all, for by its very definition, nothing *can* be done to remedy an innate and immutable condition. The function of the label in this context seems to be to locate the problem firmly within the learner rather than within the provision which we supposedly make for her. 'Dullness' is likened to a kind of chronic medical condition: in the final analysis there can be no cure, but at least we can do something to make the patient a little more comfortable. One source of confusion is precisely that such a term is used to cover a variety of 'conditions', some apparently remediable, others not. The 'backward' child, for example, is one who, according to his performance on standardized attainment tests, is not performing at a level 'commensurate with his chronological age' (Brennan, 1974, p. 20), but whether this is remediable or not depends upon the *cause* of that low performance. In the case of the 'retarded' child, the 'cause' resides in some shortfall between her attainment and what she ought to have attained in the light of her measured ability; in short, 'a condition of unrealized intellectual ability' (Brennan, *op. cit.* p. 20).

Thus, it is possible to identify five separate categories of children: those who are backward because dull; backward because dull and retarded; backward because retarded; neither dull nor backward, but still retarded; and children who are neither backward nor retarded (and therefore not 'dull' either). The fact that one word: 'remedial' can/has been used to describe such a range of 'conditions' in itself gives cause for concern for it suggests to the uninitiated the possibility of administering a similar treatment for a range of diseases. To pursue the analogy: it has the dangers of a diagnosis that does not differentiate between asthma, bronchitis, pneumonia and smokers' cough — since all are in some way 'respiratory disorders'.

The 'initiated', of course, don't make such errors, but in avoiding them may only make matters worse. The addition of a category like the 'slow-learner', for example, only adds to the confusion when a standard definition of the term does not exist. For Williams (1970,

p. 9), the 'slow-learners' are 'those children of limited intelligence' (that is, the 'dull'), for the DES (1971) they are 'children of any degree of ability who are unable to do work commonly done by children of their age' (that is, the 'backward'), while for Brennan (1974, p. 16) they are a mixed bag of retarded children of average ability, together with the mildly dull (some of whom are also retarded). More recent coinings, for example, the 'specific learning disabled' and those with 'special educational needs', don't necessarily help much either, since they suggest either that the whole 'bag' is even more voluminous than was thought, and/or that each need is after all so 'specific' as to confound all attempts at generalization.

Two further assumptions can be seen to underpin these various formulations. One is that the development of cognitive abilities is roughly commensurate with what 'academic' education is about: that the measurement of ability is to do with attainment in a traditional academic curriculum in which the basic skills are those of reading, writing, numeracy and remembering (Gurney, 1976, p. 13). The other is that education is to be seen essentially as a matter of comparison and competition: one's classification in terms of the kinds of category discussed above is, after all, a matter of how one scores on tests which have been 'standardized' against the performances of others of one's own 'age' (whether chronological, mental, or whatever). The whole idea of education as centrally concerned with an academic curriculum in which the norm is *not* the full development of the self, but what is 'normal' for some 'generalized other', is one which dominates schools' attempts to provide for specific categories of kids and which, as Gurney (1976, p. 25) has shown, has a distorting and unhealthy effect.

Attempts to be more sophisticated in our thinking about special needs of one sort or another have, of course, been made. Westwood (1975 p. 16–17), for example, has distinguished between five categories of such education: 'adaptive', 'compensatory', 'remedial', 'therapeutic' and 'special', while others (for example, The Plume School, Maldon [1973]) have written of 'adaptive-developmental', 'corrective' and 'remedial' education, and as a series of descriptions and surveys (for example, Thomson *et al.* 1974, Sampson 1969, Sampson and Pumfrey 1970) show, schools have adopted a variety of organizations and strategies in attempting to meet such needs. But two things still seem to be the case: one, that some notion of relative ability to achieve in the mainstream curriculum is at the root of such provision; the other, that a shared set of problems confront the school in its attempt to make such provision. These problems can be summed up in a number of key questions:

1 How may children with learning difficulties be best catered for in the context of prevailing notions about education and ability, and prevailing organizing principles (selection, grouping by ability, examination goals)?

2 To what extent does assistance with such learning difficulties require the help of professional experts, and to what extent should such assistance be given by the 'ordinary' teacher in the context of normal classes?

3 What is the relationship between the work of the 'remedial educationalist' and the work of other teachers with a responsibility for the 'welfare' of the child (including the pastoral care specialist)?

4 How does a school identify and separate children with special needs in order that they can receive the kind of help they need without labelling and stigmatizing categories of children in ways which are not merely unhelpful but actually counter-productive?

How teachers in two schools have perceived these problems and tried to come to terms with them is described in the next section.

Both schools are mixed comprehensive schools in catchment areas containing substantial housing estates for the London overspill, the clientele of School A being of rather lower 'socio-economic' status than that of School B, but both having a substantial proportion of children from lower working-class homes. School A, in the ribbon of dock and industrial development along the Thames, was formerly a secondary modern school, and with its eleven to sixteen year old age-range, retains many of the characteristics of its earlier status. Children finishing their fifth year may proceed either to the sixth form college or to the technical college, both of which are close to the school.

School B, in a pleasant rural town some forty miles from London, has very different origins. Purpose-built some seven years ago as an eleven to eighteen comprehensive, the school is entirely on one level (to accommodate the envisaged integration of the disabled) and has a very large open-plan area, with sliding wall-panels to provide for various combinations of space. With falling rolls, the school has had to share its sixth form with the town's other comprehensive, teaching being provided in a sixth form centre on a campus two miles away. In fact, both schools suffer from falling rolls — School A has declined from eight forms of entry to five, with a further decline feared, while School B has had to shed at least two full-time teaching posts (by natural wastage) in the last year.

As a visiting researcher, I found the atmosphere of the two schools markedly different. School A was very reminiscent of secondary moderns I had taught in in East London: not a uniform to be seen beyond the first year, a policy of rigorous exclusion of children from the buildings at 'break', evidence of vandalism to lockers, walls etc, and a general feeling of depression about the place. School B, by contrast, struck me as warm and inviting. Every child — and even the odd teacher! — wore uniform, all floors were carpeted, there was no visible vandalism or grafitti, and a striking freedom of movement was permitted to all throughout the day.

If it is legitimate to talk about a school's overall philosophy or policy, then in this respect also, there were contrasts. In School A, a weak preference for mixed-ability teaching, at least in the early years, had been established, but beyond that it was very much up to the individual subject departments to group as they wished. This was legitimated in a rhetoric of 'independence' and 'autonomy' which barely concealed the existence of deep divisions of opinion between (and sometimes within) departments, and a somewhat anarchic and constantly changing pattern of grouping from one year to the next. Something of a core curriculum existed, and there was some attempt at integration of geography, history and religious education into 'humanities', but here again there were 'separatist' pressure-groups within the constituent departments. Officially, but again rather ineffectually, it was policy not to use the label 'Remedial' to describe the department in whose work I was particularly interested, with 'Basic Skills' being the preferred title. As well as the head of department, there was a second teacher working full-time and a third teaching about a quarter of a time-table on Basic Skills. The full-time staff occupied adjoining rooms at the end of a corridor of home economics rooms, quite remote from the English and maths departments to whose interests the work of Basic Skills was most often seen as relating.

In School B, the mixed-ability principle had been central to the founding headteacher's philosophy and in the context of building an institution from scratch, was one she had managed to develop in the majority of the school's work. However, there were 'weak-spots' — notably modern languages and to some extent mathematics — where substantial groupings by ability took place, and it was clear that elsewhere in the curriculum more-or-less informal 'settings' occurred. None-the-less, the degree of consensus amongst staff as to the un-desirability of selection generally and streaming in particular was considerable, and stands in stark contrast to the laissez-faire elements of School A. A similar contrast existed in respect of the integration of subjects. In School B a flourishing and well-designed humanities course taught to three classes at a time in the open-plan area, and using key-lessons and work-sheets in a thematic approach, was a feature of the curriculum. As in School A, School B had eschewed the label 'Remedial', but with greater vigour. To mention the word in my early visits to the school was to leave me feeling that I ought to go and wash my mouth out with soap and water! The preferred title here was 'Supportive Education', and the Supportive Education Department was generally seen as an essential and significant part of the school's provison, with two full-time members of staff and a head of department filling a Scale Four post for this and his house-head responsibilities. A further member of staff had recently been appointed to the department to run a special withdrawal unit for children with serious problems of an emotional or behavioural nature, and together the accommodation for the department comprised a suite of three rooms, centrally located in the complex.

The choice of labels in both schools is a demonstration of concern over the stigma that has all too often come to be associated with the 'remedial' child. Both heads of department feared the effects of identifying and extracting a particular group of children for special treatment, both as a potential exercise of the self-fulfilling prophecy and as an actual exercise in labelling: they were genuinely concerned that other children would ridicule such youngsters with name-calling and exclusion from in-group activities. To some extent this did still happen, but in School B the incidence of this seemed negligible.

Both heads of department were perceived by staff and children alike to be helping children primarily with English and mathematics, but this was seen as only a part of the picture by the teachers themselves. In School A, the head of department saw herself as very much involved in compensating for the cultural deprivation of one particular estate in the catchment area. She had, herself, established through testing the measure of 'linguistic deprivation' in the area, and, informed of her findings, many other staff could articulate the similarity of the profile of their children's reading ages to those of inner-city schools. But she was also concerned with reversing a poor self-image produced by previous labelling, and compensating for a perceived lack of social and interpersonal skills which she attributed to home background. That she did this in a sympathetic and unpatronizing way was very clear from the children I interviewed, but it is less clear how other teachers acted on the information she gave them. And it is true that the second in her department shared neither her definition of an educational 'need' nor her approach to Basic Skills teaching. For her, the 'basics' really *were* the basics: however dressed up in topic work or whatever, this teacher's concerns were exclusively the development of reading, writing and numeracy, preferably in a regular one-to-one withdrawal situation, apparently oblivious to the problems of labelling that this might entail. In any event, most remedial work was done by all Basic Skills staff in the context of stable and regular (if small) 'bottom-stream' classes for English, maths and such alternative syllabus subjects as 'communication skills'.

This was not the case in School B. Here, the concept of the unequal distribution of talents within a child (rather than *between* children) was the dominant organizing principle. Thus it was argued that *any* child might have a problem with some aspect of ordinary school work and that this was by no means an indication of the child's level of 'general ability' across a variety of tasks. Much was made, for example, of the child whose attainment was good in all subjects but had a problem with handwriting or spelling. Nor were relevant skills seen as exclusively the 'basics' of literacy and numeracy — help with skills in drawing graphs and reading maps were also mentioned as examples of the support the department existed to give. While some of these services were provided through regular twenty minute workshops of two or three children, in spelling, reading and handwriting, the bulk of the department's work — and its raison d'être — lay in the help it gave to children in 'normal lessons'. In humanities in particular, a member of the Supportive staff was involved as a 'floater' — a fourth teacher circulating amongst the three classes in the open area, helping any child with a problem on the worksheet, and in the process indentifying candidates for workshop provision or helping *in situ* youngsters with problems of which the department was already aware. That *any* child might ask for and receive assistance from the floater *or* from one of the class-teachers was a further and impressive way of avoiding the labelling of those who might well have been in a permanent 'bottom group' had they attended School A.

As in School A, the Supportive Education teachers saw the problem as more than simply an 'academic' one. There was a considerable overlap between children who might have been defined as a 'pastoral' problem, a 'discipline' problem or an 'academic' problem (*cf.* Best *et al.* 1983 Ch. 10). But whereas in School A, the head of department held no position of pastoral responsibility and saw herself as regularly going beyond her brief of 'Basic Skills' in providing moral support, guidance and socialization to her children, in School B this problem was alleviated by having the head of department as one of the three heads of house. This permitted easy communication with other pastoral staff — his fellow heads of house and the deputy head (pastoral) — and to some extent avoided the dubious division of a child's learning difficulties into understandable but contrived categories.

Both heads of department had clearly been influential in developing the awareness and sophistication of staff in regard to the kinds of problems with which 'remedial education' is normally associated, yet the message was different. In School A, it was to alert staff to the *general* problems which a whole category of children were held to suffer: the 'culturally deprived' of a particular sector of the catchment area, and to offer both advice and accurate measurement of the problem. In School B, it was to assist in the development of alternative materials (worksheets etc) and to provide a consultancy service on the best way for ordinary subject teachers to meet the needs of individual children while the 'specialists' themselves worked in 'the field' alongside them. In both schools there were avowed fears of labelling and stigmatization, yet in both schools some element of this still existed. Indeed, it is difficult to see how the provison of a specialist service is possible without something of this being the case. In School B, we may well have observed the most that is possible, yet even here the rhetoric that 'every teacher is a supportive teacher' could not totally neutralise the effects of a reality in which some professionalization of 'support' is inescapable.

What these cases show — and this is particularly true of School B — is that the old concept of 'remedial education', pervasive though it is in many respects, can no longer do justice to the realities which some schools are creating in their attempts to cater for those with learning difficulties of one kind or another. None-the-less, there are still problems which no change in nomenclature alone could resolve. For even in School B, the rhetoric could not conceal the fact that the real problems were, in the last analysis, perceived as the failure of some children to fulfil the requirements of an academic curriculum. Whatever was said to the contrary, everyone knew that it was literacy and numeracy which were the key skills to be developed, and that it was the academic subjects of English, maths and a portmanteau of others ('humanities') which took most of the time and energy of the specialists. In other subjects, help was either not forthcoming or was substituted by the creation of an alternative (low-status) subject usually devised and taught without advice or assistance from the specialists: 'modular science', 'natural science', 'European studies', and 'design for living' courses for example.

This raises questions about the hidden curriculum of remedial provision generally, for in offering a smattering of academic pursuits in a watered-down curriculum (as in the case of at least one teacher in School A), or in concentrating on literacy and numeracy (the case in both schools), the validity of the 'mainstream' curriculum is confirmed and prolonged. And that means that the differential evaluation of different kinds of pursuits is also perpetuated — the academic subject versus the practical subject — and in the process we continue to create two classes of pupil and two classes of citizen, the same two with which this article began.

In short, those whose welfare requires that they receive 'special' education of some sort or another are seen to be failing in the kind of education which is really valued. The fact that this is an education which offers them little of perceived relevance, is at odds with the indigenous culture of the area, and undervalues those intersts and skills which they do have, is all too often overlooked. The result is that education is not truly 'comprehensive' at all: we do not accept the diversity of skills, talents and interests which that title conveys. Nor, therefore, can we value equally the diversity of children for whom we cater. As Daunt has argued (*Comprehensive Values* 1973), the principle of equality of opportunity is not enough, for it accepts the value of scarce objectives (academic success) for which children are expected to compete, rather than asserting the principle of *equal value* in which the development of any individual must be cherished as much as that of any other. Moreover, as Hargreaves (1980) and Williamson (1980) among others have argued, the attribution of the problem (whether academic or pastoral) to the child effectively distracts attention from the failure of the mainstream curriculum of our schools to provide a set of meaningful and relevant learning experiences for a substantial proportion of our youngsters. The 'ideology of pathology', as Golby and Gulliver (1979) have called it, conceals the truth about the illness of the system itself.

However it is clear that things are more 'healthy' in some schools than in others. While by no means perfect, School B does provide an example of an institution in which the traditional orientation of remedial education has been replaced by the provision of support for those who need it in a context of a broadly progressive philosophy which includes mixed-ability teaching of an integrated curriculum in an open-plan setting. Moreover, the various *kinds* of support which pupil-welfare entails are also to some extent integrated in the dual pastoral/academic roles of key staff. And as both schools show, a thoughtful and dedicated head of department can wield considerable influence in changing and developing more humane and enlightened attitudes towards the variety of problems for which we all, from time to time, need support.

That such efforts are unlikely to lead to a revolution in the curriculum as we know it, or to the overthrow of the stratification of activities within it, should not cause surprise. The historical and social forces for the maintenance of the academic status quo through the self-fulfilling measurement of ability and attainment are too strong for that. But that, it seems to me, is another and altogether larger battle, a battle to be waged in the halls where overall educational policy is formulated. At the time of writing, such revolutions seem far away indeed.

In the meantime perhaps the most we can hope for is a conception of education in which the old category of the 'remedial child' can be exploded for the social construction that it is (Davies 1980), and replaced by a commitment to the worth of each child's development in the context of an integrated system of support.

School Welfare and Pupils with Special Educational Needs

Neville Jones
Principal Educational Psychologist, Oxfordshire

Introduction

The terms 'welfare' and 'special needs' currently play an important role within our educational vocabulary. They give rise to a range of expectations and responses, not all of them educational and by no means all rationally articulated, at the level of meaning and of practice mongst teachers, within schools and upon a wider educational and social canvas.

'Welfare' can be seen to embrace not only some notion of personal and institutional value which finds expression in a written, spoken, or practised philosophy, appropriate or otherwise, to the declared intentions of the 'embracer', but also a more public and prescribed meaning. For some, the concept of 'welfare' is related to those attributes which the *Oxford Dictionary of English Etymology* describes as being in a state of 'well being' or of living happily, but of course these are not solely the prerogative of those children who, in another sense, receive welfare help. For others, 'welfare' is normal schooling, is something that occupies space and time between the activities of the ordinary curriculum. 'Special needs', however, may be described as those disabling conditions of minority groups of children who, being difficult to teach in normal school environments, are set apart in special units and schools where they are 'out of sight and out of mind'. Welfare is something extra but takes place in the ordinary school. Special needs, however, are often thought of as something that takes place elsewhere. Children with educational needs, through a formalized procedure of identification, assessment and classification, have been deemed to require something additional,

139

that is, something special, and by definition, therefore, something not in ordinary schools.

For purposes of both welfare and special needs children tend to be seen as having needs that are peripheral to the main reason why they are in school — that is to learn. But experienced teachers will recognize that to some degree what has been described above are stereotypes of old concepts of welfare and special education. What has to be recognized, however, is that, whatever changes have come about in the last decade associated with the integration movement, the starting point for any change is from a set of notions, not always consciously or willingly acknowledged, concerning attitudes towards handicap (Jones, 1980), notions that teachers have about learning styles of children (Jones, 1984), the effective size of learning groups when balanced between group and individual learning (Burstall, 1979), and historical notions of normality (Jones, 1983), all of which dictate current practices and future formulations.

One idea, now receiving some belated attention sees 'welfare' and 'special needs' as being additional to or an extra dimension of the normal provision of the school (Sayer, 1981). This is not to assume that schools should institutionalize two quite distinct regimes, for the 'normal' and for the 'special', but rather that teachers should recognize that pupils have many and different educational needs. Were such a policy to be implemented curriculum provision would be just as specific to the needs of the gifted or disruptive child as to the pupil who is average at everything. Furthermore, 'gifted' and 'disruptive' would not be regarded as separate categories. What, then, is it in the present system which calls for such extra time and commitment?

The Extra in Welfare and Special Needs

It might be useful first to consider numbers of children. With 'welfare' needs this is always a reflection of the way a school wants to respond and what it will invest in time and resources to do this. In relation to children considered to have 'special needs' then there is some factual information but the picture becomes increasingly blurred where schools have tried to make a response to the integration philosophy and develop curriculum policies to consume their own special smoke. But there are those children who have been processed and attend special classes and schools. Of the twelve categories of children with handicaps who are shown in the DES. Return of 1977 for England and Wales, these covered some 177, 117 pupils (1.97 per cent of the total child population). In Scotland, for the period 1976–77, the figure was 15, 119 pupils (1.4 per cent). It has been suggested that these figures represent not the real need in schools but the special school places available. National surveys, carred out by the National Children's Bureau, where some 17,000 children born in a single week in March 1958 have been followed up into adulthood, (Pringle, Butler and Davie, 1966), by Rutter and his colleagues in the Isle of Wight (Rutter, Tizard and Whitmore, 1970) and some Inner London boroughs (Rutter *et al.*, 1979), have given credence to the belief that the needs of children are closer to those put forward in the Warnock Committee Report of 1978. Here it is estimated that 'the planning of services for children and young people should be based on the assumption that about one in six children at any one time and up to one in five at some time during their school career will require some form of special educational provision' (para 3.7: see DES, 1978). Is this the extent of the 'extra' that teachers in ordinary schools have to provide if such needs are to be met?

The DES figures cover an enormous range of needs. Some are needs that will persist throughout a child's life like blindness, some forms of deafness, and severe physical handicap. These children are but a small group even counting those who go to special schools and do not compare with the two groups of the maladjusted and those with mild or severe learning disorders. These two groups constitute some 76.8 per cent of those ascertained as needing 'special education' in special schools.

Also one school's maladjustment is another school's norm and adjustments are made to accommodate this where it arises. Furthermore, intellectually dull children are not slow learning in every aspect of their daily lives unless, of course, they are in home or school environments that expect them to be so. If maladjustment is defined as a condition having the characteristics of being 'severe, persisting and complex', it might be that all these features are open to moderation, if not cure, so maladjustment becomes a shifting phenomena that embraces both the condition as internal to the child and the response of a particular school to that condition. It is because of this that the planning for the management of maladjusted pupils who remain in ordinary schools is so difficult for the LEA administrator. But this does not lessen the time and energy that the staff of ordinary schools have to put in to cope with behavioural disturbance in ordinary schools.

It does not follow, however, that because a child has a handicap that this will disable him in the learning situation. Because of the tremendous developments that have taken place in the design of hearing aids, coupled with a strong movement by some parents and teachers of the deaf to encourage oral communication, it is now a fact that more partially and profoundly deaf children attend ordinary schools. Their priority need may not be their deafness at all but for someone to monitor daily that their hearing aid is working properly. If a key to deaf integration is hearing aid maintenance then why, where deaf children attend ordinary schools, do we not ask physics teachers to carry out this function as part of their normal work in schools? If it is a question of expertise then the physicists are likely to be the people who understand best the dynamics of hearing and audiometry. So why not use this normal resource especially if this can be backed up by a small amount of in-service training linked to such centres as the Department of Audiology in Manchester. It can be seen, therefore, that extra time is a notion that needs careful examination and no longer is it appropriate to equate resources to handicap when what we are really thinking about is handicap outside ordinary schooling and not part of normal whole school responses. The change that takes place when children's needs are met within ordinary schools, rather than in segregated accommodation, is one that moves away from handicap seen in the context of a medically classified set of disorders. Instead of implications for skills and services to diagnose, treat, and remediate, there arises an emphasis on educational management, and this calls for a different framework within which to make responses (Barton and Tomlinson, 1981).

Cut-Off Points and Boundaries

Teachers may well ask the legitimate question as to whether in the management of children with 'welfare' or 'special needs' there are cut-off points for pupil exclusion from ordinary school life. What is it that is likely to determine where the boundaries lie? The answers here are still being sought. For example, in Oxfordshire there have been three schemes by heads of special and ordinary schools to seek out alternative ways of managing children with 'special needs', under the old system of classification, within ordinary schools. In some parts of the County children previously known as educationally subnormal (mild) have been fully integrated into mainstream schooling (Jones, 1983); children with severe physical handicap are educated in ordinary classes (Jones and Southgate, 1983); and thirdly, children with severe mental retardation have been geographically integrated in a primary and its associated comprehensive school (see Booth *et al.*, 1983). These are examples of children returned to ordinary schools from special schools though here this chapter is concerned with the integration that takes place by children not being segregated out in the first place. But if there is not a cut-off point that excludes altogether, is there one that sets aside certain children *within* ordinary schools? Here we have to consider the notion of the average child where the myth of whose existence still exists in the minds and practices of teachers who teach to this average norm amongst children. Clearly children in ordinary classes have varying cognitive skills, they vary in the rate and style of their learning, there is a differential around the motivation to learn. If we make the group size large enough then there will be common factors but too often the bright children are left to set their own learning targets, and some become bored, while the slower pupils never keep up, and are largely ignored. The coherence and cohesiveness of all this is only possible given that certain children with particular intellectual, physical, and behavioural characteristics, are excluded. The educational psychologist will usually oblige to provide the well established practice of establishing the lower cognitive level fixed around an IQ of between 75 and 80; the behavioural boundary is usually determined on a questionnaire (such as the Rutter Teachers' Questionnaire or the Stott Social Adjustment Guide), or by the clinical judgment of a psychiatrist; and medical conditions remain with the doctor and his system of classification. There is little doubt that market forces begin to operate here and especially so if special classes have already been set up to take in a required number of pupils (Southgate, 1984).

In spite of the scientific approaches of the behavioural psychologist and medicine the system does not always work scientifically. If disruptive children are found to have low IQs then it is more than likely that they will end up, not in schools for the maladjusted where innate dullness is not seen as responsive to psychotherapy, but in schools for the mentally dull where their emotional needs are seen as artefacts and not central to their educational needs. Tomlinson (1981), however, has shown that there is another dimension that is, that quite able children can find themselves in schools for the mentally dull.

Teachers become aware that certain criteria are used to determine the existence, or otherwise, of certain conditions, and that such ascertainment can produce some extra resourcing. One effect of this is that the extra resource has the effect of de-skilling the class teacher and guarantees a trickle of the same problem, with the consequent further requests for more help. This is seen too often with children who have reached the magic age of seven years when full reading skills have, it seems, to be acquired. From then onwards reading becomes of less interest to the ordinary class teacher but of increasing interest to the extra specialist remedial teacher (and sometimes psychologist and neurologist). The child is then part of another system of education with teachers designated 'special', carrying out special remedial work, with special curriculum material, and some-times in special centres called reading centres. In spite of the fact that there has been found to be very little correlation between children being taught to read and their ability to read, great emphasis is placed on a style of reading teaching that is derived from teaching the severely mentally retarded, namely, behavioural objectives teaching. A prime example of this is the recently published curriculum document of the DES called *English from Five to Sixteen* which the Editor of the TES referred to as 'an astonishing mixture of the obvious, the trivial, the meaningless and the barmy'.

In spite of schools and teachers making protestations that they teach to the Bullock theme of language across the curriculum it is often very difficult to find evidence of this. Much time is spent learning to read material that has very little to do with what is con-textually meaningful for the child. So there is an inevitability that the child becomes one of those 'out of the system' as other members of his peer group, who have learned to read through what has been appropriate for them to read, move on to work that demands sophistication in reading. Hence, the demand for more and more remedial or special needs teachers to complete a job that ordinary teachers could achieve given a flexibility of approach to children. The general cut-off point for additional help is twenty-eight months below chronological age on a norm-referenced reading text, although reading tests vary in their focus and target and do not test the same area of difficulty. Most are too general to assist the design of an individualized profile and programme.

Welfare and Special Needs: A Paradox

Whatever attitudes are taken towards children needing a 'welfare' or 'special needs' response in ordinary schools, it may be the case that common cause may be enjoined in the general principle that all children, as of right, ought to have as open access to a normal curriculum as is humanly possible, that is, an entitlement curriculum.

It has the corollary that to be treated as normal is likely to maximise the possibility that those so treated will respond to normal living conditions and pressures. But what is normal? Throughout the centuries we have put outside normal society those who, because of their colour, clothing, behaviour, race, sex and opinions, are different. We have institutionalized this practice by making some children 'special' while leaving others 'normal'.

The 1981 Education Act sustains the dichotomy: special and normal now find a new vocabulary in those children who are 'statemented' and those who are not. The problem put in its simple form is how can we make a response to those who have 'extra' needs without at the same time creating conditions that exacerbate their extra needs over and above what their disability demands. We can remind ourselves of the procedure: we identify, assess and clarify, according to some criteria that ensures certain kinds of outcome. We train certain individuals to do this task more efficiently than if they were untrained. We refine our knowledge through sharing it via the organizations we set up to propagate the discipline: we publish journals and the findings of research — money is specially allocated by government for these purposes. We make special accommodation available and keep it warm, clean and maintained. In the past the recipients of this response have been given special names: the 1981 Education Act has attempted to collapse these into some amorphous human group called 'children with learning difficulties'. There are LEA advisers and administrators whose job it is to oversight the structure and there are government inspectors specially designated to ensure that the structure is well budgeted and humane.

One effect of the 1981 Act has been to increase special needs LEA administrators, advisers, and psychological services by ten per cent in personnel, yet none of this ensures in itself that a single child will have a more open access to the ordinary curriculum, nor be regarded and responded to as more humanly normal. More does not necessarily imply better, and with some of the unimaginative attempts at integrating special school children it could mean worse. It has been said that in relation to the above regarding special education it has now had its day, but what we are about to observe is a repeat performance of the exercise, with almost parallel characteristics in relation to children requiring 'welfare' help in ordinary schools, and the pastoral epidemic is nearly upon us. To say what has been achieved, through the integration movement, for example, is little more than an exercise in the reshuffling of our prejudices, is to belittle tremendous work of individuals in many LEAs. But where are the LEAs who have policies, and who put them into practice, in such ways that they do not get caught up in the paradox of providing more to make a response to those who need extra, but with outcomes that are more divisive for more children than before? It seems likely that the responsibility for an appropriate move forward here must come from the heads of ordinary schools. But what have they to help them?

The 1981 Education Act was drafted as a response to some of the recommendations of the Warnock Report. Its primary aim was to encourage LEAs to come forward with help for those requiring some extra response in schools. Aimed at the lethargic and indolent LEA it embraced for the first time in special legislation a legal, if somewhat tentative, caveat centred round parent rights. It has its own built-in paradox of being promotional legislation without any resource commitment by central government for its promotion. In essence then it is a set of procedures whose legal authority has yet to be challenged. It says nothing about most of what has been discussed in this chapter. For the most part, and as far as heads of ordinary schools are concerned, it could be safely ignored without repercussion. But in practice this minor piece of legisation has been fully grasped by LEAs to represent not a partial response to children's needs but *the* response to this area of education. It is unlikely that those who drafted the Act gave thought to this but it has been grasped willingly by those who wish to extend the 'institution' of a special response to those in special schools to a vast population of children now in or- dinary schools who will find themselves coming within the umbrella of those outside the ambit of the ordinary child. As a consequence of this there has been a large increase in the number of peripatetic specialists, mainly drawn from those who previously were called remedial teachers, who now enjoy new titles such as 'special needs advisory teachers' or have been institutionalized into support groups like those developed in the Coventry LEA (Muncey and Ainscow, 1983) and elsewhere. Many of these schemes draw strongly on procedures developed by psychologists for use with the severely mentally retarded and within a framework of objectives teaching which in relation to reading has been found to be of little use (Lawton, 1984). Possibly the flaw in so much of this work is that it is instigated by those 'expert' in relation to children who have been segregated out from ordinary schools that is, special advisers, special teachers, and educational psychologists, and its target audience are teachers in ordinary schools. Nowhere do we find production of contextually appropriate learning for ordinary teachers by *heads expert in the curriculum and management of ordinary schools.*

Welfare and Special Needs: Static and Flexible Dimensions

What has been sketched out above are some of the parameters of the organizational systems of 'welfare' and 'special needs' as they eixst today. They touch on aspects of the beginning of a journey and the nature of the baggage we are taking with us: they suggest a possible projection to what might be at the end of the line assuming of course, that all are agreed to travel and that there are no special concessionary tickets to go elsewhere. The task is first to examine in a little more detail those factors that inhibit any movement, or where there is mobility, where it appears that the route is circular. Secondly, to examine growth points that may possibly lead to 'welfare' and 'special needs' being taken out of the baggage-van trailing as it does at the back of the train, and being incorporated in the normal compartments where, it may be hoped, everyone can face and travel with some harmony towards a common destination. Before this can happen we need to examine aspects of 'welfare' and 'special needs' that are 'static' in practice and those where 'flexibility' ensures the possibility of movement forward.

The Role of Individuals

So far we have considered 'welfare' and 'special needs' as service styles that are discrete entities making their own idiosyncratic responses to different groups of pupils for different reasons and purposes. This is surely not the case. Children in both categories become the concern of the class teacher, tutors and year head: both categories will be embraced by specialist services like school counselling, social work, careers, though not all children with special needs will necessarily be seen. Some children with special needs are likely to be referred directly to outside 'agents' like educational psychologists. If, however, it is the policy of the LEA to make a 'statement' about children in ordinary schools by virtue of the 1981 Education Act, then the senior management of the school will be involved, that is, the head or his deputy. Three groups of children emerge: those receiving welfare or special help, and those receiving both.

The issue, however, is slightly more complex than the above paragraph suggests. Children who have behaviour or learning problems change gradually as they 'progress' through school. Class teachers will respond across their own individual range of skills until they have exhausted their repertoire of response, and in the process may refer a child to a senior member of staff, tutor, or specialist teacher. What dictates the style of this response may well be the laid down rules and procedures in a given school. Some children, for example, go straight into a class for 'less-able pupils' 'the first day of their secondary career because of the result of some disputable test scores: this may be their learning environment for the rest of their school days as they are caught up in the 'special' net on the first trawl. In this respect a school determines its cut-off points for certain children even though there is growing evidence that within staff groupings in comprehensive schools there are teachers who can teach less-able children, together in mixed ability classes, as well as any other child. In one monitored account it was found that what determined whether less able children were taught alongside children of differing abilities was the teachers' attitude towards the label 'less-able', or more familiarly ESN(M), and not the question of teaching skills *per se*. (Jones and Berrick, 1980).

This raises the question of consistency amongst teachers and how far what happens is basically a reflection of this. Why is it that the maladjusted child, for instance, is not maladjusted in all learning contexts of a school life, in all classes, with all peers and adults? Does the child 'select' his target for displaying his poor adjustment or does it become manifest in a particular kind of context where others are involved?

There is a growing literature on the over-riding effects of teacher choice established in a hierarchy, on which category of child they feel able and willing to teach where special needs are concerned. These differences in attitude and approach amongst a group of teachers are, of course, proving grounds for disruptive children who exploit these differences and add to the confusion. Some may claim that it is the differences in teacher attitudes that add the extra dimension to what may already be a state of insecurity within a child.

Sometimes the question is asked by a teacher — is he maladjusted? And the question is double-edged. For some teachers it means that if he can be ascertained as maladjusted they take him away: for other teachers the label secures a confidence to request extra help and guidance — the label functions to meet a need, consciously or otherwise, in the wishes of the teacher.

In all this there is a range of choices being exercised and sometimes laid down procedures of action do not allow for an exploration of choices by groups of teachers. At first sight it would appear that teachers cannot win. If it is argued that formal procedures are essential for stability in a school then it would appear this inhibits choice making, and vice-versa. In either situation the situation is in some way a static form of response in a school. Both situations lead to a rigidity in the sense that there is little or no growth from either poisiton. What is being postulated is that necessary structures are derived from choice-making and that within these structures are the elements of their own change so that as circumstances change and new solutions are found to old problems so it is possible for new structures to emerge.

Static and Flexible Dimensions of Welfare

Welfare carries some general concept of caring and this in itself can mean that there is little expectation that the pupil makes a contribution to the joint exercise of exploring situations. The extra element is time to set aside for a meeting to take place and where this is part of the daily timetable of a school it becomes a measure of the relative importance of the activity as such by pupils and staff alike. But welfare can be seen in a number of 'static' ways:

1 *Welfare reinforces the perception of a child as being weak or vulnerable:* The placing of children in full-time classes for the less able is an example.
2 *Welfare creates a relationship of dependency* and the task is seen by both teacher and child as one of continuing support.
3 *Welfare is associated with the distribution of largesse*: The days are not passed when this could simply mean money and clothes but educational largesse can mean making available to the child other facilities within the school as a response to the child's needs. These could be a referral on to a school counsellor or special needs teacher, or to outside agencies.
4 *Welfare is only for a small group of children:* Children receiving welfare help form cohorts in a school and to this extent they are seen by others as special groups and not as individuals whose needs may in some respects differ from those of others in the school community.
5 *Welfare tends to be a crisis response*. The crisis arises often because the children's individual needs make them more difficult to teach in ordinary classes as presently constructed. One effect of the crisis response is to make a rigid distinction between such children and others so that they become 'welfare children' instead of children who, among their educational needs, have welfare needs.

6 *Welfare is not preventative*. This happens because too often the welfare response is of a particular kind, that is, it may be related to the establishment of discipline. The task here is to support the discipline procedure and not to explore why for a given child discipline issues arise. Hence, the issues that apply to one child might well apply to others but the welfare intervention that is static in its response makes no response to wider issues in the school.

A flexible welfare response has built into it a set of negotiations that extend beyond the issue that first brought about the welfare exchange between teacher and pupil. Welfare in this sense, while not replacing the subject areas as the engine room of the curriculum, though as a notion this has yet to be explored and would be a viable part of the exploration exercise, might look to its flexible nature in terms of 'a moving set of relationships within which different groups of individuals are constantly in negotiation' (Measor and Woods, 1984). All the time there are reflective processes taking place on why, for instance, the curriculum timetable is as it is, or why the discipline system works in a certain fashion and does it work effectively in this form. So there are set pieces within a school: its stated aims and objectives; the structure of teaching groups; the content of the curriculum; the welfare system that also embraces a response to children with special needs. But is there a matrix of organization that gives rise to 'the moving set of relationships' that will allow a school, in its corporate sense, to continually carry out the task of individual and institutional self-evaluation. This is the dynamic for growth of child and adult alike and it concerns itself not with what is happening today but what indications there are for change for tomorrow: therefore, we are talking about the process reflecting on the content and product of the present. If welfare is to be a flexible component of this process then it has to clearly be located in the curriculum, not in terms of 'other activities', but as a complementary act of learning situations parallel to and interactive with every subject area. It is suggested that in its dynamic sense it is located in areas of pastoral care, careers, the pastoral curriculum, and the personal and social development of pupils. More specifically this will cover the following:

1 *Pastoral care*: (a) Tutoring (b) Counselling (c) Parents (d) Discipline and reward (e) Outside agencies (f) The wider community (g) Its structure and roles

2 *Careers*: (a) Guidance in (year three) (b) Guidance out (year five) (c) Careers education (d) Work experience
3 *Pastoral Curriculum*: (a) Tutorial periods, years 1–5 (b) Personal and social education
4 *Personal and Social Development:* (a) Independence and decision making (b) Communal life (c) Behaviour, initiative and responsibility

There is, therefore, the marrying together of 'attitudes and relationships' with the 'organizational structure' so that both move from being static precepts to on-going processes involving individuals in a never ending set of consulting experiences with others related to what is contextually relevant for every person involved in the time they spend in school.

Static and Flexible Dimensions of Special Needs

The historical tradition of placing children with special educational needs in segregated provision, units or schools, where they would receive a 'special' kind of education ear-marked by small teaching groups, a lowered expectation for learning, a therapeutic style of education for the maladjusted, and a grouping together of children with the same handicaps to cover an appropriate special curriculum, has thrown up new problems of management where more of these children are now retained in ordinary schools.

One style of management that has been imported into British schools from America is that of the Resources model (Jones, 1981). This is an exceedingly flexible style that meets most of the criticisms currently aimed at special education in special schools. It involves schools having resource bases (rooms and equipment) and it operates on a 'levels of intervention' principle. For any given child with handicaps the task is to enquire whether there are ordinary lessons the child can partake in without extra help; whether there are lessons where something extra will be required (i.e. equipment, teacher skills and knowledge, a specialist support teacher to help with team teaching, or an extra pair of hands provided by a welfare assistant); and which lesson periods the child will need to be withdrawn to the resource base for an alternative curriculum, special training, or basic skills work. Such an arrangement maximizes a child's experience of the normal but at the same time makes a concession to his special educational needs.

Some of the aspects of a welfare response in school have been touched upon above under the headings of vulnerability, dependency relationships, largesse, crisis treatment, and prevention. What are the static and flexible aspects of these elements of the welfare response that are pertinent to children with special needs and their management?

Clearly children with special needs are vulnerable because that is what the term means. But care needs to be taken that we do not increase that vulnerability by managing them in such a way that they do not extend their talents by the fact that we minimize expectations for reaching goals which their handicap suggests may be unreachable. Placing children who are known to be in the intelligence range seventy-five to eighty-five IQ in special classes where they remain for the rest of their secondary schooling is a case in point. These children function well in a resources style of management described above.

Dependency relationships characterize the management of children with special needs as much as those seeking welfare help. This is sometimes due to learning in early life when the handicap has encouraged an attitude of over protection by parents. Sometimes what is required here is not so much shoulders on which to cry but what the Quakers would call 'stern love': in counselling terms the encouragement to face reality.

The term largesse is used loosely here but if it is taken to mean being offered something for nothing returned then too often children with special needs find themselves in this situation. Any interaction between adult and child, if it is to be at all therapeutic and growth producing, requires demands to be made and obligations entered into. Sometimes with adolescents this means that actual contracts require to be made for some future behaviour and follow-up to ensure that it takes place. So often interviews are of a passive nature, a listening ear and a sympathetic manner, yet adolescents, still finding boundaries for their own emotional growing, require something more structured and concrete.

Although crisis situations do occur with children with special needs, especially the disruptive child, it is often the case that such pupils have put out signals long before the crisis happens. To this extent the crisis is not child-centred but community centred in that not enough people concerned with the child noticed what was happening, felt it important enough to do something, or as is likely, knew what to do. Flexible management of disruptive pupils means that teachers have to know precisely what to do if caught in a crisis and where to seek help: these episodes then cease to crisis so much as moments of optimum stress when children experience that those concerned for him can also handle positively extremes of behaviour.

Whatever action is taken by teachers to help those with special needs there must be part of it that forestalls similar difficulties in the future. Sometimes this is achieved by feedback systems to classroom staff and moreover their continued involvement in the child's problems. It is very easy for a specialist to take over a child's problems leaving the class teacher deskilled on this and future occasions.

A special problem arises with disruptive children who are placed in off campus units. The older disruptive may simply be ready for work but the law does not allow this: the younger disruptive a therapeutic experience that will eventually take him back to successful learning. If 'work' and 'therapy' are part of the normal curriculum for this group of pupils, because they use and capitalize on the opportunities these methods provide, then why can they not be part of the normal curriculum in ordinary schools? This may require some specially designated room space, in the same way that the sciences, woodwork, pottery, and physical education require designated room-space, and their own specific forms of equipment. The off-campus location of these units has two effects: it takes the problem away from the ordinary school and from teachers who originally had responsibility for the pupils, and it does not prevent the trickle out of mainstream schools of such pupils. Secondly, pupils are aware of their segregated circumstance. Yet this is the time in their lives — as young people who will probably marry earlier, experience pregnancies, be unemployed, and have to cope with work and money, more than most others — when the building up of self-esteem is at its optimum. There is no doubting the quality of some of the therapeutic work in these units (White, 1980) but the exclusion process has placed these youngsters in an even more vulnerable position in their self appraisal of themselves *vis-a-vis* the society in which they live.

The Whole School Ethos

Research studies are indicative that it is the ethos of a school that is the main factor in deciding academic and behavioural achievements and outcomes (Reynolds, 1976). But ethos is a concept that does not lend itself easily to analysis.

In considering the welfare and special needs of children in a school this chapter has explored the notion that ethos operates at two levels. First, in terms of the attitudes towards handicap as expressed through styles of 'welfare' and 'special needs'. Secondly, through the network of services that provide and respond to them, and the practical outcomes. This part of the ethos is considered in its 'static' mode. Also, there are attitudes, services, and solutions that have built into them a *flexibility* that reflects the 'relationship' mode outlined by Measor and Woods.

The flexible mode is not child-centred but concentrates on interactional experiences that are growth propelling for both pupils and teachers. It has an element of creative self-evaluation but is focused towards others in whatever grouping the child or teacher finds himself. It has a dynamic element that is derived from the personal interactions but carries an implication for planning a structure of arrangements for individuals to interact. To this extent it is not a passive concept and does not permit a 'wait and see what happens' philosophy. Its emphasis is on inclusiveness and to this extent it has a particularly important part to play in the way that services for children requiring welfare and special education are developed.

Schools and the Things That They Do to People: Towards a Welfare Orientation

Keith Blackburn
Headmaster, St George's School, Gravesend

Introduction

The experienced pastoral head (see Blackburn, 1983a, 1983b) is used to intervening in the lives of pupils to bring about change. Unacceptable behaviour and poor work-rate are the usual spurs to action. In addition there are pupils with problems — educational, vocational and personal — to whom advice, counselling and support may be offered. More recently the notion of enabling pupils — all pupils — to cope more effectively with school has come to the fore. This latter focus divides itself into two closely related questions. What experiences are we to provide for pupils which will enable them to cope more effectively? What experiences are pupils gaining from their participation in the institution of the school which may be helping or hindering their capacity to cope effectively?

The development of pastoral curricula has been one response to the first of these questions. As teachers have become involved with enabling pupils to develop study skills, to discover ways of relating more effectively to other people, to develop a sense of their own identity and to develop the capacity to respond appropriately to other people so new dimensions of these questions have emerged which have to do with the attitudes, values and working styles of the members of the school staff. Faced with a problem the pastoral head may seek solutions within the three lines of thought already delineated — the control of behaviour and work, meeting the needs of an individual pupil with a problem or looking to develop the pastoral curriculum — as a way of helping pupils to respond more effectively. Whatever their merits, all these solutions focus upon the pupil whereas, in some cases, at least, an effective response may entail bringing about changes in the attitudes, values or working styles of teachers.

My concern in this paper is to illustrate ways in which I have observed such processes at work in schools and to suggest ways in which those in leadership roles may seek to bring about the necessary changes. My sense is of the tip of an iceberg. There is much to discover and understand. This is but a beginning. A beginning which will focus initially upon a number of specific cases of which I have some knowledge. The cases are real but the schools and individuals involved have been suitably disguised.

Some Illustrations

1 Northlands School

Northlands School has been through a process of change. Once a secondary modern school it is now a comprehensive school. Several of the staff in senior roles have been there for a long time. Such staff changes as have occurred have been among those in more junior roles. From a career point of view by standing still some staff were effectively promoted through comprehensive reorganisation but as the years have passed they have come to realize that if anything they may have been over-promoted and have, in any case, now reached their ceilings, yet they have some years of service before retirement. In the transition period following comprehensive reorganization their primary concern was to demonstrate the school's capacity to achieve well in external examinations with the more recently acquired able pupils. A traditional approach to teaching was adopted in which teachers with secondary modern experience were able to concentrate on quality and content in the pursuit of success; wider questions of curriculum development were not raised. This has given rise to a conflict within the staff group. Younger teachers, particularly those who came to the school to start their teaching careers, have found themselves unable to put into practice the methods to which they had been introduced in their training. New ideas have generally been blocked in discussion, it being felt by senior and well established staff that a successful formula has already been adopted. In this context bringing about changes in the classroom experiences of pupils has meant the covert introduction of unofficial innovation and the teachers involved have been aware of the possible conflicts that might arise if their actions were discovered. Internal examinations anyway impose a considerable constraint on any such variation in classroom work.

Some pupils have gathered a sense from some of their teachers that what they are doing is far removed from what it could be and this has been reflected in the attitudes and approaches of such pupils to their work. The extent to which particular pupils have been affected by this attitude has varied according to the exigencies of the time-table. What is clear is that some pupils have been more exposed to it than others. Furthermore, the staff are barely conscious of the operation of this process in the school. How, asks the pastoral head, can we improve the attitude and the performance of John Smith? To a great extent it would seem that it is John Smith's teachers rather than the pupils who may need to be the focus for his attention. That is to say that it could be that senior staff, who may recognize the need for change, may yet be asking the wrong questions and of the wrong people at least some of the time.

Similar processes and issues may arise in schools whenever changes are made. The introduction of new content, of new teaching methods or of new pupil groupings may well all give rise to conflict. There will be those who embrace the change with enthusiasm while there will be others who resist it. What will always be true is that the attitudes adopted by teachers will affect the attitudes of pupils.

2   Moorlands School

The Senior Master at Moorlands School prided himself on the control and order that existed in the school. Come rain, hail, snow, storm or tempest no pupil would come onto the school site before the start of the school day. Apart from its religious content, Assembly was an opportunity for him to have a few words about some aspect of the school's routine and to remind pupils of the consequences of deviance. His style reflected that of a regimental sergeant-major. Persistent patrols during the day and an efficient detective service meant that few — he claimed none — ever got away with anything. At the end of the day the school was re-assembled to witness the public identification of the day's miscreants and the announcement of the punishments. The Senior Master was readily available throughout the day — even when teaching — to deal with any problem pupils. The school was perceived, by some at least, to run efficiently.

From the point of view of many pupils the school day was an

experience of fear — fear that they might transgress one of the school rules and be subjected to the consequences. In the main the majority of pupils were never in trouble but this required a lot of nervous energy to make sure that they 'kept within the law'. At the other extreme there were those pupils who had been in trouble so often that it had become part of their way of life, while others had slipped into patterns of absence which enabled them to avoid the situation. For the majority school was a tiring, unpleasing and stressful experience. The outcomes of being schooled in this context were not known. But what was clear was an absence of the excitement and enthusiasm for learning amongst pupils that can be found in some places.

Equally, the school that gives little attention to order and control creates a situation in which pupils may well experience disorder, even chaos, in their relationships with their peers and with their teachers. Little learning occurs here either. Most schools reflect a compromise position somewhere between the two polar extremes that I have described. Furthermore, within any school there will be individual teachers whose attitudes and practices stand at different points of the spectrum between these two extremes. Somewhere in the middle is the optimum situation in which there is sufficient order for work to proceed effectively while at the same time enabling pupils to flourish in their learning. Within any particular school there will be a variety of views about where this middle position lies.

As the pastoral heads reflect on how they might assist their pupils to succeed they may need to start by looking at what teachers are making pupils feel about themselves if their experience of school is to be changed.

3   Homework

Homework provides a further illustration of ways in which adult attitudes and responses may affect the pupils' experience of school. It is common for a school to have a policy on homework, to provide a homework timetable and possibly a homework diary for pupils. Parents may have been told when their children joined the school that homework would be set regularly and their support was sought in providing a quiet place for their child to work and in helping when the task set was not understood. The response of some teachers is to meet these expectations by regularly setting and marking homework. Some teachers from time to time and some regularly set homework but do not mark it. Pupils may come to feel that there is little point in putting themselves out to complete assignments well. Some teachers from time to time and others regularly set tasks for homework which are effectively non-tasks. 'Complete classwork' may be an example of this. Some teachers simply do not set homework.

For the pupil there is a conflict in his experience. From some sources he is told that homework is an important part of his learning. From other sources the practice does not square with this belief. It must be either that homework is not really important or that while it is important for some pupils, for him and his peers it is not a worthwhile process. 'We are not up to serious work.'

The pastoral head may exhort the pupil to take his homework seriously but he will not be 'heard' while the pupil is receiving counter-messages from other sources. Once again it may be that it is the teacher and not the pupil who needs to be in focus if change is to be brought about.

4 *Attitudes to the Worth of Different Kinds of Educational Experience*

The value system in some traditional grammar schools was to spot-light academic achievement, particularly in examination terms. The number of pupils gaining University places was seen as the chief measure of success. Some secondary modern schools used a parallel process of evaluation. For them the measure of success was the number of pupils who, despite their failure to gain a place in a selective school, had been successful in achieving 'O' level passes and had been able to proceed to sixth-form education.

It can be argued that the idea of the comprehensive school called such goals into question, insofar as the notion of comprehensive education was based upon the fundamental principle that each pupil's education should be regarded as of equal worth (see Daunt, 1975). However laudable is the expression of such a commitment it is of little value if it is not reflected in the practices of the school, the attitudes of its teachers and, most importantly, into the experiences of its pupils. At one level the school can take account of what it writes about itself in its handbook or in the way it handles the issue of examination certificates. Much more subtle and important are the attitudes which teachers express in their daily dealings with their particular pupils. The exhortation 'if you work hard enough you too can pass "O" level' — an impossible goal for some — is an all too common way of attempting to motivate pupils. Conversely, 'The description of CSE as a "Certificate of Second-class Education"' reflects an attitude that pupils learn unconsciously from some of their teachers. It is instructive to look at what happens when timetabling constraints make splitting a class between teachers a necessity. 'We can't split them, they're "O" level'. Arguably the needs of the less able demand consistency of teaching; the more able are likely to be more capable of coping with shared teaching in a subject.

Taking the point of view of the pupil, teachers need to ask the question 'What am I made to feel about myself and the way that I am valued here?' This question can be asked of the school generally but needs also too to be asked in relation to the particular teachers that a pupil meets during the course of the school week. Pupils who are parallel by ability may have very un-parallel experiences in school in this regard. The pastoral head reflecting on pupils' responses to school may catch a glimpse of what it must be like to be pupils in this school and may, once again, conclude that the situation will be helped forward by focusing on the staff rather than on the pupils as the place where change needs to be sought.

5   Some Sketches of Staff

My last illustration comprises a series of sketches of members of staff. Who a person is at any given time is reflected in the work that he or she undertakes in school and in the effects that he or she has on the pupils.

'Chris' joined the school as a probationary English teacher and was from the start very good. During her next three years she built on her initial experiences and was increasingly contributing to departmental planning and preparing materials for use in school. She was keen to work in a comprehensive school and believed that such schools should be made to be good schools. More recently a new member of the department has arrived who has taken her place as the source of 'good ideas' and Chris has lost some of her enthusiasm for her task and this is reflected in the way her pupils are now responding to her.

'Jenny' joined the school as a Scale 2 teacher and is determined to make an active career for herself in schools. She is good at teaching, willing to take on additional responsibilities and uses both her evenings and holidays to take part in in-service courses. Her confidence has grown enormously since she began teaching and while she had once had an image of herself as a basic classroom teacher she has come to realize that she is capable of making a much greater contribution.

'Ann' works part-time to enable the demands of the family budget to be met. She 'calls in' to teach her classes at the appropriate times, and is gone. She marks regularly but is simply not in school to follow up pupils whose work is inadequate. As a teacher she lives on the stock of ideas that she had gathered when she was teaching full-time. As a person she is a little resentful about having to work at all and feels that as a part-time teacher she gets the classes that others don't want. These feelings reflect in her dealings with her pupils.

'Colleen' has been in one sense or another in her present school for over a quarter of a century. She started as a language teacher in a small girls' grammar school. 'They used to wear gloves.' This school was amalgamated with a boys' grammar school in the mid-1960s and then with a secondary modern school in the 1970s to from a comprehensive school. In essence her working style has remained unchanged through the years. She was able to make some attempt at coping with the boys but has never come to terms with teaching the wider spread of ability in the present school. She presents a dilemma. She can teach able pupils, but parallel groups taken by other teachers tend to do better than her classes do and her colleagues feel that they do not get a 'fair share' of the work. Her A level teaching lacks lustre. She declares often that there is no point in less able pupils taking languages — she means the bottom eighty per cent — and an 'experiment' a few years ago in asking her to teach a good CSE group was a disaster.

'Barry' is also a long serving teacher in his school. He qualified in art but some years ago, to meet a crisis, he took on the teaching of mathematics and has taught this ever since. He is well organized in his teaching and marking and pupils do well with him. However, he does not plan to alter his working routine and certainly does not wish to give any more time to his working task. As the vogue for meetings and discussions has grown in his school he has demonstrated a reluctance to take any active part in it or to be affected by it.

'Steven' is the present informal leader of his school staff room. Recently a new headteacher has arrived and a good many of the staff are for the first time in their professional experience being led by someone younger than themselves. The new head's arrival has proved to be a watershed in the careers of a number of the teachers. They had been working happily with the expectation that in due course, and as shoes became vacant, existing staff would be promoted. This expectation has vanished as posts have been advertised and external appointments made. Steven is the focal point for opposition for those who feel that their comfortable world is crumbling around them. From the point of view of the pupils much of the opposition spills over into the classroom situations in which these staff work and while the pupils do not understand what it is about, they have gathered a feeling of discontent, of disquiet and of divided loyalties.

To these brief sketches could be added many others. The point is that the attitudes and practices of different staff to a greater or lesser extent shape responses in their pupils in which some of these responses encourage creative and constructive attitudes amongst pupils whilst others do not. What these sketches try to illustrate is, as with all the illustrations I have offered, that the effective pastoral head is as likely to be engaged in the business of changing the attitudes of staff as in changing those of pupils.

Courses of Action

'Towards a welfare orientation' implies, for me, planning and acting in school in ways in which pupils are able to maximize the worth of their schooling experiences. I have illustrated various ways in which the responses of teachers may make this difficult to achieve and I am arguing that in order to achieve 'a welfare orientation' in a school it will be necessary to tackle issues that are raised by the ways in which some teachers contribute to the school.

There are two key difficulties in facing the issues that I am raising. Firstly, the attitudes, values and working styles of teachers and the effect that these have on the pupils are probably the least explored and least understood of issues relating to schooling. There are also issues which those in leadership roles in school least want to tackle. It has proved difficult enough in many places to move from problem-centred pastoral work towards strategies for helping pupils to cope more effectively in school implied in the concept of the pastoral curriculum. Whilst, in many schools, there has been much staff support for these developments there has also been much opposition. The problem for leadership is to know in what ways it might be possible to raise issues with staff so that change occurs. The second difficulty arises from the fact that the management of change is often envisaged in a utopian way as if the proposed innovation was taking place under 'ideal conditions'. But ideal conditions are rarely to be found in practice and most innovations in most schools need to be carefully planned and managed, to be paced so that the people most affected by them are able to adapt with confidence. To press too quickly causes defences to rise which will often hinder or frustrate the proposed change. Conversely, the amount of time thought of as available for change should not be regarded as unlimited and it may not be possible to carry all staff before implementing an innovation.

When and how might firm leadership cut through the delays and defences which are likely to plague any proposed change? Delays, which although they might create certain short-term difficulties, may also lead, in due course, to improvements in the ways in which all children experience schooling. It is not possible to offer general recipes, rather such questions can only be answered in the context of particular schools. But they are questions which need to be asked. In the past it has been not unreasonable to look for new appointments to the staff of schools to bring about the kinds of changes identified above. After all, in due course *all* members of staff will leave and be replaced. In more recent times a number of factors have combined to diminish the plausibility of such a strategy. Thus the reduction in the opportunities to move to new posts, for promotion on the one hand and the increasing demands that are being made on schools to adapt and change make such a passive strategy increasingly inadequate and unacceptable. Clearly a more active approach is needed. An approach in which leaders in schools have to look to processes within the school which can be used to raise questions about attitudes, values and working styles in ways that facilitate change. In particular, I want to focus on four such processes — meetings of staff, the annual report, staff appraisal and the day-to-day contact between leaders and team members as ways through which changes might be encouraged (see Blackburn, 1983a).

1   Meetings of Staff

It is common for staff meetings — of the whole staff or of sub-groups — to focus on the concrete, to exclude the exploration of more general issues and to be assemblies of people a few of whom will have already adopted a stance before the meeting begins and of those who will decide on their viewpoint largely on the basis of the particular people advocating a course of action.

It is possible for the process of a meeting to be thought out and managed in such a way that the views, opinions and attitudes of participants are expressed, in which they have the opportunity to hear what others think and feel and to be exposed to the real possiblility of reviewing and of modifying their own position.

The process that I have in mind will be familiar in a slightly different guise to those acquainted with the methods of active learning (see Baldwin and Wells, 1979–83). Such an approach was developed for pupils. It involves getting them to talk with each other in pairs and in fours along the lines raised by the leader's pre-planned agenda. As this discussion takes place the pupil learns something of what he or she thinks and feels about the issues raised. The act of speaking is very often an act of discovery; until this point the pupil may not have formulated his or her view. Hearing what others think enables pupils to compare and contrast their own view with that of others and it is in this process that the individual is exposed to the possibility of choosing to change. The role of leader is to enable the process to take place in such a way that members of the group can come to their own conclusions. What it is not is a means of providing, at the end, the 'correct' solution or answer.

This kind of process can also be applied effectively to meetings of teachers. It will involve considering the physical setting in which the meeting is to take place so that it is conducive to the hoped for interaction. It will involve considering the agenda item for discussion. 'The First Year Syllabus' for example is likely to be treated in a 'content' way. 'What do we feel that we are trying to achieve in the first year?' invites a different kind of discussion in which there are no obvious content answers but members of the group have to tackle underlying themes and issues. Similarly items such as 'Uniform' or 'School Rules' also invite content responses, whereas, 'What ought we to expect from our pupils in terms of their behaviour?' invites a wider discussion in which views and attitudes can be expressed. The process works best with teachers when the group is broken into sub-groups for the first part of the discussion, the sub-groups being small enough for each member to be able to speak. At a later point sub-groups can convene to hear the various views that have been expressed. It is in this second phase that the leader becomes involved in the discussion. During the course of the discussion a variety of thinking will be seen and conflicts may be expressed. For success the group must feel that the leader and the led are fellow-explorers of the issues raised — it is not a softening-up exercise before a view is 'sold' to them. The effectiveness of the process can increase with use and it can provide an effective agent for exploring and changing attitudes and values in a group and helping teachers to consider their working styles.

It is increasingly common for schools and for departments within schools to set out their aims and objectives. The discussion of these, using the processes that I have described, can be an opportunity for such teachers to experience a different level of working together.

2 Annual Report

In structure an annual report reviews the progress that has been made by a group of teachers during the course of a year, attempts some evaluation of successes and failures and sets objectives for the coming year. It is comparatively easy for a leader to write a report on his own. However, the report can be an opportunity for discussion among his team. The group can be asked to contribute ideas and themes that ought to be raised in the report. They are able to contribute their views of the successes and failures during the year and to setting of objectives for the coming year. Once drafted the report can form a second opportunity for discussion. The process can provide an opportunity for staff to discover more of what they think and feel, compare their views with those of others and choose to adapt to change.

3 Staff Appraisal Interviews

The structure of an appraisal interview can be parallel to that of a report — review, evaluation, goal-setting (see Blackburn, 1985). Here the teacher is able to talk on a one-to-one basis about his work and the way he feels about it. Hopes as well as fears may be expressed, difficulites articulated and successes acknowledged. The teacher has the opportunity to check on his or her course and perhaps may choose to make modifications in attitudes, values or working styles as a result of new insights gained. Held at regular intervals, perhaps each year, the interview can be an increasingly important tool in enabling leaders in school to participate in the professional development of the teacher as well as being a further agent of change within the school.

4 The Day-to-Day Contact with Staff

It is the style of some leaders to send memos to staff requesting — or telling them — what they would like done. I have argued that the day-to-day contact with the staff who form the leader's team is an essential tool in enabling such leaders to fulfil their role effectively

(Blackburn, 1983a). In face to face contacts it is possible for the leader to be much more aware of the nuances of a teacher's response. By using some of their counselling skills leaders can encourage individual teachers to express themselves more fully. He or she may be able to help such teacher to think through issues a little more fully or to see other aspects of the situation of which they had not been previously aware. He or she may be able to help clarify attitudes and values, pointing to differences and enabling these to be acknowledged. It may be an opportunity to empathise with difficulties that the teacher is experiencing in school or beyond. Handled with skill the day-to-day contact with teachers is an important agent for change.

Conclusion

Each of the processes that I have described and advocated above depends for its success on three assumptions. Firstly, that leaders are prepared to be changed themselves by the processes. It is an aspect of leadership to identify issues that need to be explored. The leaders are likely to have thought their way through towards a number of possible solutions and may have a preferred way forward. The processes that I have described encourage and enable teachers to allow their defences to drop a little and to become vulnerable as they express themselves. To do this trust has to be built so that the processes can become effective. Trust arises from mutual exchange and sharing. To use the processes to sell ready made solutions rarely serves to bring about changes in people. The second assumption is that a better solution is likely to be achieved by people working at problems together. The participants are more likely to have an involvement in the effective implementation of the solution if they have shared in the teaching and planning. A third assumption is that there is a lot of energy available in the staff of a school. This energy is often used in pursuing widely divergent attitudes, values and working styles. The more that energy can be harnessed to the successful pursuit of implementing the aims and objectives of the school the better will be the school experience of the pupils.

Schooling and the Maximization of Welfare

Hywel Thomas
University of Birmingham

Introduction

While education is clearly a complex activity, its final significance for individuals can be described in quite simple terms. For those individuals involved in educational activity it provides a mixture of present and future satisfactions and dissatisfactions, and the net balance over time of these satisfactions and dissatisfactions can be formulated as the sense of benefit and well-being which individuals draw from their educational experiences. It is this net balance of benefit and well-being which is defined here as welfare, a definition which is significantly wider than is used in many other chapters of this book and it is to be hoped that the ensuing analysis will be evidence enough to justify this distinction. The chapter will focus principally upon educational experiences within a single sector, compulsory secondary schooling, with the practical purpose of exploring ways and means of maximizing welfare benefits within that sector. However, although the analysis will concentrate on this one sector, the analysis could also be fruitfully applied to other sectors of educational provision. Indeed the analysis will draw upon practice in the primary sector as a possible guide to activity elsewhere.

In outlining the structure which the chapter will follow, it is necessary to begin by recognizing that there are diverse groups, with strong interests in education, who may also have differing welfare preferences. It would be understandable, for example, if many employers took the view that the most satisfying educational provision was one which emphasized the link between education and work, so that school leavers were better prepared for that world, even if it meant that provision was less effective in terms of assisting children to enjoy their non-work time. It might even be the case that preferences not only differ, but are quite incompatible. Thus, if one group of teachers and parents preferred children to leave school having the ability and the desire to question the social structures of our society, this would be incompatible with the desires of another group of teachers and parents who might prefer children to leave school with enthusiasm for the existing social order. These differing and even incompatible preferences pose problems in any attempt to consider the maximization of welfare from schooling, as they entail choosing between the preferences of different groups. They will be problems considered in this chapter within the format described in the following paragraph.

The analytical framework for examining the problems of max-imizing the benefits of education begins by recognizing the character-istics of education as a 'consumption good' and an 'investment good' (explained below), and that the value of one of these characteristics as against the other differ for groups and individuals. It is an analysis which will be applied to the two groups principally involved in secondary education on a day-to-day basis, secondary school chil-dren up to the age of sixteen, for whom the welfare benefits and dis-benefits of schooling have life-long implicatons; and their teachers, who are prepared to commit a working life of up to forty years to schooling. The attitudes and expectations teachers bring to work, and the net balance of welfare which they take away from it, is clearly an important influence on the quality of the process. Now this suggests that other important groups with an interest in and influence on education will be excluded, such as parents, employers, churches, higher education. However, they will not be neglected in the analysis because in examining the consumption and investment nature of education for children, it will in fact be necessary to take some account of the interests and preferences of other groups. This will be evident in the following section which discusses the children and the maximization of their welfare from education.

Children and the Maximization of Welfare

For children, education is both a consumption good and an invest-ment good. It is a consumption good in those circumstances where an activity contributes directly to welfare because it is a part of education which children value for itself. This may arise because activities provide immediate pleasure where children, for example, simply enjoy their lessons as they take place, but it is also a consumption good in those circumstances where present educational activities are productive of future satisfactions; for example, where skills of map reading are used on a holiday excursion with parents or, even many years later, when the children of today use their skills with their own children. The pleasures and satisfactions which arise from education as consumption can also take the form of the pleasure of struggling with complex problems and mastering difficult skills. Education as consumption is not to be confused with education as a sequence of saccharine lollipops. Education is an investment good in those circumstances where it is acquired because of its capacity to be converted into something else, from which welfare-yielding experiences are obtainable. This conversion process of investment education into consumption benefit is usefully illustrated. For many children mathematics lessons may be archetypal investment education, studied not for any immediate or future pleasure but in order to obtain an examination certificate of prime importance in securing direct access to employment, or to employment following other educational experience. The income obtained from employment enables individuals to purchase goods and services of their choice, completing the process of converting their investment of time and effort in mathematics lessons into welfare-yielding consumption.

The conceptual distinction made here between education as consumption or investment is, hopefully, clear enough, but difficulties arise as soon as we begin to use these concepts to analyze the likely nature of the experiences of children. Many children enjoy their mathematics lessons and also value them as an investment activity, obtaining the bonus of simultaneous consumption and investment benefits. For other children, there is no constancy in the nature of the welfare yield of parts of the curriculum, where history, for example, may be enjoyed when it is taught by teacher X and loathed when taught by teacher Y. Some other children may gain no pleasure from their immediate educational experiences but still do well in examinations, and draw from the investment of time and energy into education welfare-yielding high status jobs and good incomes. However, analyzing this untidy reality using the distinct and distinctive concepts of education as consumption and investment leads to important questions about the nature and implications of the compulsory schooling sector with which we are familiar.

First, to the extent that education is regarded as a consumption good which people value for its own sake, and given the assumption that children as consumers are capable of rational decision-making

concerning their own self-interest, the notion of compulsory schooling entails circumstances where we are forcing an individual to
consume a commodity designed only for their pleasure. This does not
mean that children do not actually exercise choice, although its nature
requires clarification. While children play little part in decisions on
the content of the curriculum they are to be offered, they have a
crucial role in the process of converting curriculum inputs into
outcomes. The choices made by learners can include rejection of the
package (truancy), apathy (lack of attention in class), ineffective
commitment (failure to comprehend) and effective commitment
(successful completion of teacher determined objectives). Learner
choice is crucial for curriculum outcomes but is given little influence
in determining the quality and range of curriculum inputs on offer.
Such limits on the available choices of children might be defended on
the basis that education is a rather special 'merit' good, the benefits of
which are appreciated only after it has been consumed. In this
framework, education is something that people ought to consume
whether they *anticipate* liking it or not. To allow complete choice of
what, when and how education is to be consumed is to run the risk
that children will make the wrong choices, rejecting existing compulsory schooling provision. Stated in this extreme form makes some
anxieties about choice legitimate, but the alternative to existing
restrictions on choice is not to abandon all limits, but is to reduce
restrictions and broaden choices. Moreover, we do well to recognize
that the choices of children are affected by the preferences of others,
notably parents but also the child and parent's view of the expectations of employers. In other words, it might be expected that, even
giving children more choice would still lead to a demand for much
that is conventionally found in the curriculum. Of course, the
argument for increasing choice if education is only a consumption
good must be particularly forceful, but it applies just as much when
we analyze the implications of recognizing that education is both a
consumption and an investment good.

An immediate consequence of recognizing the consumption and
investment duality of the education process and product is that we
have to consider the relative significance of one as against the other.
This presents itself as a problem in two principal ways, one related to
education and the allocation of time and the second related to the
impact of a child's subjective valuation of one facet of education (say
consumption) on the same child's subjective valuation of its other
facet (investment). These are discussed in the next two paragraphs.

With regard to education, the allocation of time and the relative importance of education for consumption and investment, we do well to remember that, even during an individual's employment lifetime (i.e. setting aside childhood, pre-employment preparation and retirement) non-work time amounts to more than two-thirds of total waking time. Now any concern with the maximization of welfare must take account of the welfare obtained from non-work time activity (Becker, 1963, p. 493) and education as consumption has a crucial role in this respect, because it contributes to the use and pleasure to be gained from the allocation of non-work time. And since non-work time is such a substantial proportion of all time, it would seem appropriate to tailor much of educational provision to that part of life. What emerges from this is the basis of a powerful economic rationale for devising (or, rather, negotiating) curriculums which take explicit account of the leisure and pleasure times of children, soon to be adults. But it is only a basis, especially if we were to assume that the welfare benefits which adults draw from the allocation of non-work time is also likely to depend, at least to some extent, from their income, since the latter determines their capacity to obtain certain experiences. This assumption of an income factor on welfare leads back to the investment significance of education, because education as investment is a means of access to high status, good income employment. Does this mean that the curriculum must be guided by the investment factor in education because it may be productive of greater welfare, rather than allow the emergence of greater emphasis on consumption? It is an issue which brings us to the second problem mentioned above and is considered in the next paragraph.

The problem of how a child's subjective valuation of the consumption benefits of education affects the valuation of investment benefits can be crystallized into a simple question: does the amount by which children enjoy education (a consumption effect) affect their attitude to its investment potential, and their decisions to stay-on beyond the compulsory age to seek its investment benefits? It is a commonplace to ignore these private consumption benefits when calculating the benefits of education, on the grounds that they are so hard to measure, but Drake (1981, p. 156) is one who argues that learners, '. . . are always estimating consumption effects. They frequently allow their expectations about these effects to colour decisions about learning options which are largely undertaken for investment reasons.' If Drake is correct in attributing to consumption factors these effects on investment decisions, policy implications which emphasize learner choice emerge again. After all, what is being argued is that the immediate pleasure which children obtain from the process of schooling is crucial to their decisions of how they value the longer term benefits of education as investment. The policy implication is to negotiate a curriculum which children enjoy, not only because of the significance of education for pleasure and leisure (as argued above), but because enjoyment is seen as a crucial factor in decisions to stay-on for the investment benefits of schooling. There is, however, a potentially crippling stumbling block to such a policy which is related to any linkages between curriculum content and the investment potential of education. In order to obtain investment benefits from education, must the curriculum contain certain things, whether or not they provide children with any immediate pleasure? Let us now consider investment and curriculum content.

What is it about education which means '. . . that independently of social class and ability, education in general has been significantly and positively asssociated with the income of individuals' (Williams, 1982, p. 99)? Why is it that, '. . . expenditure on education has in the past been, and is seen to be, a worthwhile *private* investment' (*ibid*, p. 99)? This is a most important issue of current debate among economists and sociologists of education and what follows is the merest precis. Readers can obtain rather longer precis in Blaug (1983, *passim*, 25pp), Watts (1983, pp, 6–15) and Williams (1981, pp. 98–102) which provide sources of fuller statements in the debate. One explanation for the private investment value of education is that it offers relevant cognitive skills and knowledge which *prepare* individuals for certain categories of work, the higher earnings of educated people reflecting a higher productivity in employment which results from their education and training. This is an explanation which is under considerable challenge, evidence suggesting a poor match between the skills and knowledge acquired in schooling and those used in employment. Challenging this explanation is a view that the real preparation for employment takes place through the *socialization* function of the 'hidden' curriculum, which emphasizes different traits for different occupational groups. For those destined for lower level occupations, emphasis is placed on punctuality, docility, compliance; whilst the elite, who are diverted towards higher education, are encouraged to become self-reliant, versatile, capable of assuming leadership. In addition to this socialization function, education is also a *selection* process, which not only provides the labour market with a means of classifying workers into different groups but does so using an apparently fair certification process which legitimizes the income and status inequalities which follow.

Profound implications for education emerge from these alternative explanations of why education is a worthwhile private investment. With regard to the *preparation* function; if, in fact, there is no compelling link between the cognitive skills and knowledge used at work compared with those transmitted in schooling, it not only raises considerable doubts about contemporary efforts to vocationalize the formal curriculum, but also provides grounds for increasing the emphasis on education as consumption (for pleasure and leisure) and for greater choice by children on the content of the curriculum. Such a change need not be inimical to the *selection* function of education because employers seem to be principally concerned with using the certificates as a guide to their decisions in classifying applicants for jobs. The curriculum content which precedes the certification process is, for the vast majority of jobs in the economy, of little relevance. It is in relation to the *socialization* function that real problems present themselves, potentially inhibiting moves to greater choice for children and subsequent diversity of schooling provision and processes. These problems are considered in the next two paragraphs.

Those who explain the role of education in terms of its socialization function, viewing it as a means of reproducing in schools the social relations which exist at work, see much of this reproduction taking place in the so-called 'hidden' curriculum, which sends out the crucial affective messages about role and behaviour to relevant social groups. To change this curriculum would appear to present a threat to the social order, because a different sort of 'hidden' curriculum would fail to prepare children for their post-school roles. However, not to challenge and change this curriculum might stand in the way of increasing the welfare obtained by children from their schooling. This is because the 'hidden' curriculum may contribute as much, if not more, as parts of the formal curriculum to the dissatisfactions and disbenefits of schooling which reduce its net benefit for many. Here we have an example of the incompatible preferences mentioned in the Introduction which pose problems for welfare maximization: if the investment function of education is this socialization process, facets of it appear to be incompatible with the types of policies to increase the choice which is necessary to increase the welfare obtainable from consumption education. And it is of little use allowing children simply to exercise their own preferences and choose their own balance between consumption and investment education because, presumably, those who finance the education budget would not allow such choice. For them, education must continue to meet its investment obligation, socializing individuals into their appropriate occupational categories. Moreover, many parents would support such a view, anxious that their children be prepared for employment and, despite its inappropriateness, enthusiastically supporting moves to vocationalize the curriculum because it is believed to increase its instrumentality. Does this mean that compulsory schooling is trapped, having to be dominated in its form and content by this investment imperative? The answer to this is all too likely to be yes, because views on appropriate schooling seem to be deeply conservative among many parents and employers. However, it is just possible that change of a substantial nature could emerge and it is this possibility which is discussed in the following paragraph.

Is compulsory schooling at a nadir from which it is about to rise? The catalyst for such a change lies in those same characteristics which threaten a vocational emphasis to the curriculum: unemployment and the collapse in demand for many unskilled routinized jobs. The collapse of demand for these jobs signals an opportunity to move the 'hidden' curriculum of most children away from its emphasis on punctuality, docility and compliance. The value of this shift could well be recognized by employers who increasingly see the virtues of self-reliance and versatility in their labour force. What is being argued here is that, in investment terms, the characteristics of a functionally efficient 'hidden' curriculum may be changing and, indeed, that its differentiation for different categories of labour may be inappropriate. Moreover, a curriculum which is designed to encourage self-reliance and versatility might have those features of choice and diversity likely to exist in a consumption-directed curriculum. And the case for such a curriculum also arises with the growth of unemployment. The education system cannot solve the unemployment problem and it is to be hoped that its resolution lies in the re-distribution of work, allowing a continuation of the long-term decline in the average number of hours worked. Its effect of increasing time for leisure activities adds yet more weight to a consumption-directed curriculum.

What emerges from this analysis of how children might maximize their welfare from schooling? Policies designed to increase choice in the curriculum are a way of increasing the potential satisfactions of education as consumption. Similar policies might also be appropriate for the new patterns of work and leisure which may be emerging, though in relation to education as investment what is needed is first, to make the 'hidden' curriculum explicit and second, to cause it to be changed. At least two barriers stand in the way of these changes, the first of which are the welfare preferences of teachers. The second are the preferences of many employers and parents who wish to retain a traditional format to the existing formal and informal curriculum or, at best, agreeing to change only in the direction of vocationalism. Teachers have a key role in removing these barriers and they will be considered in the next section of the chapter, which begins by examining the welfare preferences of the teachers themselves.

Teachers and the Maximization of Welfare

There are many reasons why people choose to be teachers, but one important factor is likely to be that it provides the money by which teachers can acquire, for their life outside schools, those things that maximize their personal welfare. However, the work itself may directly provide welfare benefits in three principal ways. First, as Robertson (1963, p. 18) argues, '... work also ... is itself up to a point a direct source of welfare. In particular ... unemployment consists ... in loss of *status*, in the feeling of being unwanted ...' Second, the work of teaching will provide satisfaction in itself for some members of the teaching force, who would continue to teach for much lower levels of financial reward. Third, teaching is a form of employment which allows an individual a certain flexibility in terms of deciding what to do and how it might be done, and whilst this will differ as between schools and role, it exists for all teachers in some degree. It is in this area of discretion that the welfare seeking choices of teachers may not always be compatible with the welfare preferences of other groups with interests in education. How teachers sometimes pursue interests which are not obviously linked to the welfare of children can be illustrated and it is appropriate in this book to draw upon a research study on pastoral care.

In an early report of their research study on pastoral care in a comprehensive secondary school Best, Ribbins, Jarvis and Oddy (1980, p. 262) draw attention to a number of different perspectives on pastoral care as an activity in the school, expressed in five distinct languages. They conclude,

> The variety of attitudes teachers display, and the distinctive languages they use in accounting for their actions, suggest that very idea of a 'school' having a caring ethos is an unwarranted reification ... and in the final analysis it is perhaps on the level of the teacher as a *person* with a particular

personality, a particular self-image, and a host of ambitions, aspirations and hang-ups, that much of what goes on in schools has to be understood (p. 268).

In one example, a member of staff is presented as being more concerned with who controls records than with the merits of the 'pastoral' issue being discussed and '. . . a meeting of "pastoral" staff turns out to be much more informative about both the problems of administrators and the personal ambitions and aspirations of members than it does about the welfare of the children whose individual care is their especial responsibility' (p. 265). This example is not introduced in order to argue that the interests of teachers and pupils are always incompatible or that teachers pursue their own interests regardless of the welfare interests of children. Its purpose is that it warns us that we should not take for granted the motives and purposes of teachers who are, and will remain, an influential group within education.

The level of this influence leads one writer to describe education as a producer-dominated industry. He draws attention to the extent of their influence in shaping educational provision,

> Decisions as to curriculum, syllabus, and pedagogic method are taken largely by teachers. They are subject to external pressure in the form of examinations . . . and to a moderate degree by Her Majesty's Inspectorate . . . Teachers are limited by the resources made available to them . . . and there is a minimum performance requirement to do with actually turning up and doing the job in a nominally correct fashion (Peston, 1980, p. 120).

Schools could be described as command economies where a small group of resource controllers, and not the members of the economy acting in accordance with their individual preferences, decide upon the allocation of resources to different activities. The senior teachers who decide on the distribution of subjects in the curriculum and actually construct the timetable exercise very great control over the allocation of time of other teachers and the children. In the classroom, the teachers exercise very specific control over the way children must spend their time. The choice of subjects, the selection of material and method of study are opportunities for teachers to implement their own preferences. To the extent, for example, that teachers have value preferences for an education in the liberal tradition, these preferences can be expressed in the curriculum provision which they make. Such provision may be perfectly satisfactory for those who have the means and the desire to enjoy the menu, but somewhat neglected are the preferences of those not yet convinced of the merits of a liberal education.

As already explained, we must not conclude that in this command economy control over provision means control over outputs. At the process stage we have seen that children can and do exercise choices which are crucial for learner outcomes. Children retain the opportunity to reject the curriculum on offer, although with miserable consequences for their welfare. Here then we seem to have another example of potential incompatibilities between the welfare preferences of different groups, in this case teachers and their pupils. It is a case where teachers might benefit by allowing the welfare preferences of children to predominate, and the reasons for this are to be found again in those changing characteristics of the labour market.

The growth in youth unemployment and the expectation that it will remain indefinitely as a problem is creating the most profound problems in some schools. The argument that by working hard the reward of a good job will follow rings hollow for many youngsters, and its use by teachers as a device for persuading children to tolerate an unattractive curriculum, formal and 'hidden', is losing its force. Whether children react by truanting or attending to lessons in a most desultory way the welfare consequences for teachers must be poor, since they will obtain little satisfaction from such behaviour in their pupils. Somehow, conventional curricula and their justifications must be altered but, to keep the discussion within the boundary of likely alternatives, it will be assumed that comprehensive schools will be retained together with compulsory education as far as sixteen years.

The previous section of this chapter argued that welfare maximization for pupils, in terms of consumption and investment education, is more likely through policies which increase diversity and choice in schools. It is the argument of this section that, since hard work in schools no longer guarantees employment, many children are less likely to acquiesce in unpalatable patterns of schooling, thereby increasing the dissatisfaction of teachers with their work. Logically, teachers need to respond by creating more variety and choice in the curriculum. This would need to include choice over what is to be studied and how topics and subjects are tackled. This is difficult enough given resources, of which more in the Conclusion, but the pattern of managing children's time also needs altering. As with some parts of further and higher education children need more opportunities to manage their own time, studying when they choose and not be required to attend particular classes at set times. Much of the secondary sector can also learn from practice in those schools in the primary sector which structure the day in ways which give individual children opportunity to manage the order in which tasks are completed. It is changes in these areas of schooling which can contribute much to altering the 'hidden' curriculum, so that versatility and self-reliance is emphasized in place of docility and compliance.

If teachers can sponsor changes of this nature, offering parents and employers the prospect of schooling experiences for children which are more relevant and more positive, stimulating greater independence and more creativity, desires to emphasize the instrumentality of schooling and preferences for vocationalizing the curriculum will be considerably weakened. But from where can the initiative for changes such as these come and, given the problems of resources for education, are the proposals too expensive to implement? The Conclusion will consider these questions.

Conclusion

A strong lead for the curriculum and organization changes outlined here could come from those teachers with specific 'pastoral' responsibilities in schools. There are three main reasons for this suggestion. The first is that, arguably, they are better placed than many of their colleagues to see the dissatisfactions for many children with much existing curriculum provision. They can also be more involved in what Williamson (1980, Chapter 12, *passim*) has called the process of 'pastoralization', having a role in assisting,

> ... the reduction of resentment felt at the lack of opportunity offered and at the limited learning experiences provided (which) is achieved at the personal level, between tutor and pupil. It is this negative function I have called pastoralization (p. 174).

The second reason for suggesting the 'pastoral' area as a likely starting point for these initiatives is the change already taking place in this area, particularly through the use of prepared material in form periods. These activities are outside the formal curriculum and need not be bound by some of its familiar constraints. Indeed in some respects, where personal skills programmes emphasize independence of judgment and co-operativeness, they are already engaged in making parts of the school's 'hidden' curriculum more open and explicit which is an important first step in challenging practice in the more formal curriculum. Introduced effectively into schools, such initiatives could lead, by example, to developments elsewhere. However, the enthusiasts of the new personal skills oriented 'pastoral curriculum' should take care to observe the individual welfare principle underlying the discussion in this chapter. It means that this part of the curriculum also needs to be voluntary, enabling children to reject some of the provision and use their time in other ways. It would be an irony if a curriculum designed to develop independence of mind were to prevent that independence being exercised. A third reason for this area being an appropriate starting point rests in the very use of the term 'welfare' by many involved in pastoral care. It is a term which invokes a greater consideration of a child's affective needs than is suggested in much of the subject curriculum, where emphasis is placed on cognitive knowledge and skills. An obvious alternative starting point for change is in the social science/social education area, where the subject material often deals with the link between schooling and work; understandably, the changing nature of that link presents all too obvious problems for teachers.

Some of the changes which are needed entail producing more choice within the classroom and altering pedagogy and are, to a considerable extent, within the control of groups of teachers or a department. However, the more fundamental but essential changes to school organization, allowing children as much flexibility as the law will allow, requires not just passive support from heads and senior staff but a considerable commitment by them to the innovations needed. It would involve radical changes to school organization and teaching resources, and does beg the question whether they are legitimate and realistic demands to place upon secondary school teachers at this time. After all, consider this. A secondary school reflecting these ideas would place more emphasis on independent and co-operative learning by children, whose skills in such work would be developed from at least their first year in the school. More money would have to be devoted for producing and providing learning packs; books, video and tape libraries would need to be well-stocked, well-staffed and easy to access. The notion of teachers based in classrooms with varying sizes of groups through a day neatly broken into seven or eight periods would be replaced by teachers who would sometimes teach large groups but often be available for smaller numbers who would bring their problems to the teachers. It is a model which has some similarities with universities, except that there would be a greater emphasis on preparing and making available resources, and there would almost certainly be better learner support. Perhaps a more persuasive model would be practice in many primary schools. Such changes could be resourced, although it would mean progressively shifting a proportion of the education budget away from teachers and towards materials (currently at a scandalously low level) and non-teaching support. It would also mean schools being more open, drawing in support from parents and other adults (young and old) far more extensively than at present.

Threatening to the status and expertise of teachers as these proposals appear to be, weakly reflecting as they do some of the ideas of informal learning networks propounded by Illich (1971, *passim*), these suggestions actually offer teachers a way of defending their own long term welfare as an occupational group. They offer a route by which teachers can generate their own, the children's and the public's enthusiasm for schooling. It is an alternative to the retrenchment of the present and the incipient vocationalism which portends an uninviting future.

Bibliography

ACE (1980) 'Disruptive units', *Where*, 158, pp. 6–7.

ACLAND, H. (1980) 'Research as state management: The case of the Plowden Committee', in BULMER, M.J.A. (Ed.) *Social Research and Royal Commissions*, London, George Allen and Unwin.

ASSESSMENT OF PERFORMANCE UNIT (1981) *Personal and Social Development*, London, DES.

BAILEY, C. (1984) *Beyond the Present and the Particular: a Theory of Liberal Education*, London, Routledge and Kegan Paul.

BAKER, J. and CRIST, B. (1971) 'Teacher expectations' in ETASHOFF, J. and SNOW, R. (Eds.) *Pygmalion Reconsidered*, Ohio, Charles Jones.

BALDWIN, J. and SMITH, A. (1983) 'Uncertain futures: An approach to tutorial work with 16–19 year olds in the 1980s' in *Pastoral Care in Education*, 1(1), pp. 40–5.

BALDWIN, J. and WELLS, H. (1979) *Active Tutorial Work Books 1–6*, Basil Blackwell in association with Lancashire County Council.

BANTOCK, G. (1968) *Culture, Industrialization and Education*, London, Routledge and Kegan Paul.

BARTON, L. and TOMLINSON, S. (Eds.) (1981) *Special Education: Policy Practices and Social Issues*, London, Harper Row.

BAZLEGETTE, J. (1983) 'Taking up the pupil role' in *Pastoral Care in Education*, 1(3), pp. 152–9.

BECHER, T., ERAUT, M. and KNIGHT, J. (1981) *Policies for Educational Accountability*, London, Heinemann Educational Books.

BECKER, G. (1965) 'A theory of the allocation of time' in *The Economic Journal*, September, pp. 493–517.

BEST, R., JARVIS, C. and RIBBINS, P. (1977) 'Pastoral care: concept and process' in *British Journal of Educational Studies*, XXV(2).

BEST, R., JARVIS, C. and RIBBINS, P. (1980) *Perspectives on Pastoral Care*, London, Heinemann.

BEST, R. and RIBBINS, P. (1983) 'Rethinking the pastoral-academic split' in *Pastoral Care in Education*, 1(1), pp. 11–18.

BEST, R., RIBBINS, P., JARVIS, C. and ODDY (1980) 'Interpretations: teachers' views of "pastoral care"' in BEST et al. (Eds.) (1980) op. cit.

BEST, R., RIBBINS, P., JARVIS C. and ODDY, D. (1983) *Education and Care*, London, Heinemann.

Bibliography

BEST, R., RIBBINS, P. and RIBBINS, P. (1984) 'Careers Education and the Welfare Curriculum' in *Pastoral Care in Education*, 2, 1, pp. 66–77.

BLACK PEOPLE'S PROGRESSIVE ASSOCIATION (1978) *Cause for Concern, West Indian Pupils in Redbridge*, Redbridge Community Relations Council.

BLACKBURN, K. (1983a) *Head of House/Head of Year*, London, Heinemann.

BLACKBURN, K. (1983b) 'The pastoral head: a developing role', in *Pastoral Care in Education*, 1, 1, pp. 18–24.

BLACKBURN, K. (1985) 'Staff appraisal' in MARLAND, M. (Ed.) *School Management Skills*, London, Heinemann.

BLACKHAM, H. (Eds.) (1978) *Education for Personal Autonomy*, London, Bedford Square Press.

BLAUG, M. (1983) *Where Are We Now in the Economics of Education*, University of London Institute of Education.

BRANCH, C., DAMICO, S. and PURKEY, W. (1977) 'A comparison between the self-concepts as learners of disruptive and non-disruptive middle school students' in *The Middle School Journal*, 7, pp. 15–16.

BRENNAN, W. (1974) *Shaping the Education of Slow Learners*, London, Routledge and Kegan Paul.

BROPHY, J. and EVERTSON, C. (1976) *Learning from Teaching: A Developmental Perspective*, Boston, Allyn and Bacon.

BROPHY, J. and GOOD, T. (1974) *Teacher Student Relationships: Causes and Consequences*, New York, Holt, Rinehart and Winston.

BULMAN, L. (1984) 'The relationship between the pastoral curriculum, the academic curriculum and the pastoral programme' in *Pastoral Care in Education*, 2, 2, pp. 107–14.

BURNS, R. (1982) *Self Concept Development and Education*, London, Holt Rinehart and Winston.

BURSTALL, C. (1979) 'Time to mend the nets' in *Trends*, 3.

BUTTON, L. (1974) *Developmental Group Work With Adolescents*, London: Hodder and Stoughton.

BUTTON, L. (1981, 1982) *Group Tutoring for the Form Teacher Books 1 and 2*, London, Hodder and Stoughton.

BUTTON, L. (1983) 'The Pastoral Curriculum' in *Pastoral Care in Education*, 1, 2, pp. 74–83.

CENTRAL ADVISORY COUNCIL FOR EDUCATION (ENGLAND), (1963) *Half Our Future* (The Newsom Report), London, HMSO.

CHAZAN, M. *et al.* (1983) *Helping Young Children with Behaviour Difficulties*, London, Croom Helm.

CLARKE, J. *et al.* (1975) 'Subcultures, cultures and class' in *Working Papers in Cultural Studies*, 5, pp. 7–8.

COARD, B. (1971) *How the West Indian Child is Made Educationally Sub-Normal in the British School System*, New Beacon Books.

COMMISSION OF THE EUROPEAN COMMUNITIES (1983) *Reports on the Proceedings of the EEC School and Family Conference*, Luxemburg, EEC.

COMMITTEE OF ENQUIRY INTO THE EDUCATION OF CHILDREN FROM ETHNIC MINORITY GROUPS (1981) *West Indian Children in Our Schools*, Interim Report, (Rampton) London, HMSO.

COMMITTEE ON THE CURRICULUM AND ORGANIZATION OF SECONDARY SCHOOLS (1984) *Improving Secondary Schools*, (Hargreaves Report) London, ILEA.

CORRIGAN, P. (1979) *Schooling the Smash Street Kids*, London, Macmillan.

COX, C. and BOYSON, B. (Eds.) (1975) *The Fight for Education — Black Paper*, London, Critical Quarterly Society.

CRAFT, M. (1980) 'School welfare roles and networks' in BEST et al. (Eds.) (1980) *op. cit.*

CRAFT, M., RAYNOR, J. and COHEN, L. (Eds.) (1980) *Linking Home and School, A New Review*, 3rd ed. London, Harper and Row.

DAUBNER, E. (1982) 'Defied, depraved, denied or deprived: moral nature and counselling', *Counselling and Values* 26, April.

DAUNT, P. (1973) *Comprehensive Values*, London, Heinemann.

DAVID, K. (1982) *Personal and Social Education in Secondary Schools*, Longmans for Schools Council.

DAVID, M. (1980) *The State, The Family, and the School*, London, Routledge and Kegan Paul.

DAVIES, L. (1980) 'The social construction of low achievement' in REYBOULD, E. et al. (Ed.) *op. cit.*

DAWE, A. (1970) 'The Two Sociologies' in *Sociology*, 21, 2.

DEPARTMENT OF EDUCATION AND SCIENCE (1971) *Slow Learners in Secondary Schools*, London, HMSO.

DEPARTMENT OF EDUCATION AND SCIENCE (1981) *The School Curriculum*, London, HMSO.

DICK, S. (1983) *Communication and Confidentiality in Pastoral Care*, unpublished MA Dissertation, University of London.

DOHRENWEND, B. (1961) 'The psychological nature of stress' in *Journal of Abnormal Psychology*, 62, 2, pp. 294–302.

DOUGLAS, J.W.B., (1964) *The Home and the School*, MacGibbon and Kee.

DRAKE, K. (1981) 'Problems of financing an educational system based on the concept of lifelong learning' in HIMMELSTRUP, P., ROBINSON, J. and FIELDEN, D. (Eds.) *Strategies for Lifelong Learning I*, University Centre for South Jutland and the Association for Recurrent Education.

DUNHAM, J. (1976) *Stress in Schools*, London, NASUWT.

DUNHAM, J. (1981) 'Disruptive pupils and teacher stress' in *Educational Research*, 23, 3, pp. 205–13.

DUNHAM, J. (1984) *Stress in Teaching*, London, Croom Helm.

ELLIOTT, J. (1982) 'The idea of a pastoral curriculum: a reply to MCLAUGHLIN, T.H. In *Cambridge Journal of Education*, 12, 1, pp. 53–60.

ENGELS, F. (1972) *Origins of the Family, Private Property and the State*, London, Lawrence and Wishart.

ERICKSON, E. (1950) *Childhood and Society*, Harmondsworth, Penguin.

FITZHERBERT, K. (1977) *Child Care Services*, London, Temple Smith.

GEORGE, V. and WILDING, H. (1976) *Ideology and Social Welfare*, London, Routledge and Kegan Paul.

GOLBY, M. and GULLIVER, J. (1979) 'Whose remedies, whose ills? A critical review of remedial education' in *Journal of Curriculum Studies*, 11, 2.

GRACE, G. (1978) *Teacher, Ideology and Control*, London, Routledge and Kegan Paul.

GURNEY, R. (1976) *Language, Learning and Remedial Teaching*, London, Edward Arnold.

HAIGH, G. (1975) *Pastoral Care*, London, Pitman.

HAMBLIN, D. (1978) *The Teacher and Pastoral Care*, Oxford, Blackwell.

HAMBLIN, D. (1980) 'Strategies for the modification of behaviour of difficult and disruptive classes' in BEST *et al.* (Eds.) (1980) *op. cit.*

HARGREAVES, D. (1967) *Social Relations in a Secondary School*, London, Routledge and Kegan Paul.

HARGREAVES, D., HESTER, S. and MELLOR, F. (1975) *Deviance in Classrooms*, London, Routledge and Kegan Paul.

HARGREAVES, D. (1980) 'Social class, the curriculum, and the low achiever' in REYBOULD *et al.* (Eds.) *op. cit.*

HEALY, M. (1984) 'Developing a social education programme: A case study' in *Pastoral Care in Education*, 2, 2 pp. 93–8.

HIBBERD, F. (1984) 'Pastoral curriculum: Can it do the trick?' in *Pastoral Care in Education*, 2, 2, pp. 114–23.

HMI (1978) *Behavioural Units*, London, DES.

HMI (1978) *Primary Education in England, A Survey by HM Inspectors of Schools*, London, HMSO.

HMI (1979) *Aspects of Secondary Education*, London, HMSO.

HMI (1980) *A View of the Curriculum*, London, HMSO.

HMI (1982) *Pastoral Care in Comprehensive Schools in Wales*, Cardiff, Welsh Office.

HOBBS, N. (Ed.) (1975) *The Futures of Children: Categories, Labels and Their Consequences*, Nashville, Vanderbilt University Press.

HOLT, (1977) *Instead of Education*, Harmondsworth, Penguin.

HOPSON, B. and SCALLY, M. (1981, 1983) *Lifeskills Teaching Programmes Books 1 and 2*, Leeds, Lifeskills Associates

HOYLE, E. (1974) 'Professionality, professionalism and control in teaching' in *London Educational Review*, 3, 2, pp. 13–19.

ILLICH, I. (1971) *Deschooling Society*, Harmondsworth, Penguin.

JOHNSON, D. and RANSOM, E. (1983) *Family and School*, London, Croom Helm.

JOHNSON, D., RANSOM, E., PACKWOOD, T., BOWDEN, K. and KOGAN, M. (1980) *Secondary Schools and the Welfare Network*, London, Unwin.

JONES, E. (1980) *The Carterton Project: A Monitored Account of the Way a Comprehensive School Responded to Children with Special Educational Needs*, Unpublished MEd Thesis, University of Birmingham.

JONES, E. (1981) 'A resource approach to meeting special needs in a secondary school' in BARTON, L. and TOMLINSON, S. (Eds.) *op. cit.*

JONES, E. and BERRICK, S. (1980) 'Adopting a resources approach' in *Special Education: Forward Trends*, 7, 1.

JONES, N. (1983) 'Policy change and innovation for special needs in Oxfordshire' in *Oxford Review of Education*, 9, 3.

JONES, N. (1984) *Two People and a Context: Remedial or Contextual Bearing*, Report to Chief Education Officer, Oxfordshire.

JONES, N. and SOUTHGATE, T. (1983) 'Integrating the Ormerod Children' in *Special Education: Forward Trends*, 10, 2.

KITWOOD, T. (1980) *Disclosures to a Stranger*, London, Routledge and

Kegan Paul.

KOUNIN, J. (1970) *Discipline and Group Management in Classrooms*, New York, Holt, Rinehart and Winston.

KYRIACOU, C. (1980) 'High anxiety', in *TES*, 6 June, p. 12.

KYRIACOU, C. and SUTCLIFFE, J. (1974) 'Teacher Stress and Satisfaction' in *Educational Research*, 21, 2, pp. 89–96.

KYRIACOU, C. and SUTCLIFFE, J. (1977) 'Teacher stress: a review' in *Educational Research*, 21, 2, pp. 299–304.

KYRIACOU, C. and SUTCLIFFE, J. (1978) 'Teacher stress: prevalence, source and symptoms' in *British Journal of Educational Psychology*, 48, pp. 159–67.

LANG, P. (1977) 'It's easier to punish us in small groups' in *TES*, June.

LANG, P. (1980) 'Pastoral care: problems and choices' in RAYBOULD *et al.* (Eds.) *op. cit.*

LANG, P. (1982) *Pastoral Care: Concern or Contradiction*, unpublished MA Thesis, University of Warwick.

LANG, P. (1983) 'How pupils see it' in *Pastoral Care in Education*, 1, 3, pp. 164–75.

LANG, P. (1984) 'Pastoral care: some reflections on possible influences' in *Pastoral Care in Education* 2, 2, pp. 136–47.

LANG, P. (1985) 'Taking the consumer into account' in LANG and MARLAND (Eds.) *op. cit.*

LANG, P. and MARLAND, M. (Eds.) (1985) *New Directions in Pastoral Care in Education*, Oxford, Blackwells.

LANG, P. and RIBBINS, P. (1985) 'Pastoral care in education' entry in the *Pergamon Encyclopaedia of Education*, London, Pergamon.

LASLETT, R. (1977) 'Disruptive pupils: the facts and the fallacies' in *Educational Review*, 29, 3, pp. 152–62.

LASLETT, R. and SMITH, C. (1984) *Effective Classroom Management*, London, Croom Helm.

LAWTON, D. (1984) 'Never mind rules, read on', *The Observer*, 7 October.

LEACH, D. (1977) 'Teachers' perceptions and "problem" pupils' in *Educational Review*, 29, 3, pp. 188–203.

LEACH, D. and RAYBOULD, E. (1977) *Learning and Behaviour Problems in Schools*, London, Open Books.

LEMLECH, J. (1979) *Classroom Management*, New York, Harper and Row.

LING, R. (1984) 'SERP Survey of off-site units in England and Wales' in *Journal of the National Association for Initiatives in Social Education*, 3, 1, pp. 5–11.

LITTLE, A. and WILEY R. (1981) *Multi-Ethnic Education: The Way Forward*, London, Schools Council

LORD, E. (1983) 'Pastoral care in education: principles and practice' in *Pastoral Care in Education*, 1, 1, pp. 6–11.

LUFLER, H. (1979) 'Debating with untested assumptions: The need to understand school discipline' in *Education and Urban Society*, 11, 4, pp. 450–64.

LYONS, K. (1980) 'School social work', in CRAFT *et al.* (1980) *op. cit.*

MACBETH, A. (1984) *The Child Between; a Report on School-Family Relations in the Countries of the European Community*, EEC, distributed by HMSO.

MACBETH, A. (1985) 'Parents, schools and pastoral care' in LANG *et al.* (Eds.) *op. cit.*

MACMILLAN, K. (1977) *Education Welfare*, London, Longman.

MACMILLIAN, K. (1980) 'The education welfare officer: past, present, and future, in CRAFT *et al. (1980)* op. cit.

MACPHERSON, J. (1983) *The Feral Classroom*, Melbourne, Routledge and Kegan Paul.

MARLAND, M. (1974) *Pastoral Care*, London, Heinemann.

MARLAND, M. (1975) *The Craft of the Classroom*, London, Heinemann.

MARLAND, M. (1980) 'The pastoral curriculum' in BEST *et al.* (Eds.) *op. cit.*

McGUINESS, J. (1982) *Planned Pastoral Care*, London, McGraw Hill.

MCLAUGHLIN, T. (1982) 'The idea of a pastoral curriculum' in *Cambridge Journal of Education*, 12, 1.

MCLAUGHLIN, T. (1983) 'The pastoral curriculum: concept and principles' in PRING (Ed.) *op. cit.* pp. 90–101.

MEASOR, L. and WOODS, P. (1984) 'Cultivating the middle ground: teachers and school ethos' in *Research in Education*, 31.

MOSER, L. (1975) *Adolescent disturbance and breakdown*, Harmondsworth, Penguin.

MUNCEY, J. and AINSCOW, M. (1983) 'Launching SNAP in Coventry' in *Special Education: Forward Trends*, 10, 3.

MURGATROYD, S. (1977) 'Pupils' perceptions of counselling' in *British Journal of Guidance and Counselling*, 5, 1.

MURGATROYD, S. (Ed.) (1980) *Helping the Troubled Child*, London, Harper and Row.

NATIONAL ASSOCIATION FOR HEAD TEACHERS (1984) *Council Memorandum on Discipline in Schools*, Haywards Heath, NAHT.

PESTON, M. (1980) 'Accountability in education: some economic aspects' in *Education Policy Bulletin*, 8, 2, pp. 115–26.

PETERS, R. (1966) *Ethics and Education*, London, Allen and Unwin.

PLUME SCHOOL, MALDON (1973) 'The basic studies department' in *Remedial Education* 8, 1.

PRING, R. (Ed.) (1983) *Personal, Social and Moral Education*, Sussex, Falmer Press.

PRING, R. (1984) *Personal and Social Education in the Curriculum*, London, Hodder and Stoughton.

PRINGLE, M.K. (1980) *The Needs of Children*, London, Hutchinson, 2nd ed.

PRINGLE, M.K., BUTLER, N. and DAVIE, R. (1966) *11,000 Seven Year Olds*, London, Longman.

PURKEY, W. and NOVAK, J. (1984) *Inviting School Success*, Belmont, Wadsworth Publishing Co., 2nd ed.

RABOULD, E., ROBERTS, B., and WEDELL, K. (Eds.) (1980) 'Helping the low achiever in the secondary school', *Educational Review*, Occasional Publication, No. 7.

REDL, F. and WINEMAN, D. (1951) *Children Who Hate*, New York, Free Press.

REDL, F. and WINEMAN, D. (1952) *Controls From Within*, New York, Free Press.

REYNOLDS, D. (1976) 'When teachers and pupils refuse a truce' in MAN-

GHAM, G. and PEARSON, G. (Eds.) *Working Class Youth Cultures*, London, Routledge and Kegan Paul.

RIBBINS, P. and BEST, R. (1985) 'Pastoral care: theory, practice and the growth of research' in LANG P. and MARLAND, M. (Eds.) *op. cit.*

RIBBINS, P. and RIBBINS, P. (1984) *Developing a Design for Living Course at Deanswater' Comprehensive School*, paper presented at Annual Conference of Education Ethnographers on 'The Affective Curriculum' St. Hilda's College, September (mimeo).

ROBERTSON, D. (1963) *Lectures on Economic Principles*, London, Fontana.

ROBERTSON, J. (1981) *Effective Classroom Control*, London, Hodder and Stoughton.

ROBINS, R. and COHEN, P. (1978) *Knuckle Sandwich*, Harmondsworth, Penguin.

ROGERS, C. (1969) *Freedom to Learn*, Colombus, Merrill.

ROSENTHAL, R. and JACOBSON, L. (1968) *Pygmalion in the Classroom*, New York, Holt, Rinehart and Winston.

RUTTER, M., TIZARD, J., and WHITMORE, K. (1979) *Education, Health and Behaviour*, London, Longmans.

RUTTER, M. *et al.* (1979) *Fifteen Thousand Hours*, London, Open Books.

SALZBERGER-WITTENBERG, I. *et al.* (1983) *The Emotional Experience of Learning and Teaching*, London, Routledge and Kegan Paul.

SAMPSON, O. (1969) 'Remedial education services — report of an enquiry' in *Remedial Education*, 4, 1.

SAMPSON, O. and PUMFREY, P. (1970) 'A study of remedial education in the secondary stage of schooling' in *Remedial Education* 4, 3/4.

SAYER, J. (1981) 'Down and up the line of integration' in *Education*, 17 July.

SAYER, J. and JONES, N. (in press) *Teacher Training and Special Educational Needs*, London, Croom Helm.

SCHOOLS COUNCIL (1981) *The Practical Curriculum*, London, Methuen.

SKILBECK, M. 'Three educational ideologies' in E203 *Curriculum Design and Development*, Unit 3 *Ideologies and Values*, Milton Keynes, Open University Press.

SMITH, C. (1982) 'Helping colleagues cope: A consultant role for the remedial teacher' in *Remedial Education*, 17, 2, pp. 75–8.

SOCKETT, H. (1975) 'Aims and objectives in social education' in ELLIOTT, J. and PRING, R. (Eds.) *Social Education and Social Understanding*, London, University of London Press.

SOUTHGATE, T. (1984) 'Educated together' in *TES*, 14 September.

TATTUM, D. (1982) *Disruptive Pupils in Schools and Units*, Chichester, Wiley.

TATTUM, D. (1984a) 'Pastoral care and disruptive pupils: a rhetoric of caring' in *Pastoral Care in Education*, 2, 1, pp. 4–15.

TATTUM, D. (1984b) 'Disruptive pupils: system rejects' in SCHOSTOK, J. and LOGAN, T. (Eds.) *Pupil Experience*, London, Croom Helm.

TIZARD, B. and HUGHES, M. (1984) *Young Children Learning*, London, Fontana.

THOMPSON, A. *et al.* (1974) 'Symposium on remedial education in comprehensive schools' in *Remedial Education*, 9, 1.

THOMPSON, B. (1975) 'Secondary school pupils: attitudes to school and teachers in *Educational Research*, 18, 1, pp. 62–72.

TOMLINSON, S. (1981) *Educational Subnormality*, London, Routledge and Kegan Paul.

TOMLINSON, S. (1982) *A Sociology of Special Education*, London, Routledge and Kegan Paul.

WAKEMAN, B. (1984) *Personal, Social and Moral Education*, Tring, Lion Publishing.

WARNOCK, BARONESS M. (1985) *Teacher, Teach Thyself*, Richard Dimble by Lecture, London, BBC Publications.

WILLIAMSON, D. (1980) 'Pastoral Care or "pastoralization" ' in BEST *et al.* (Eds.) *op. cit.*

WATTS, A. (1983) *Education, Unemployment and the Future of Work*, Milton Keynes, Open University Press.

WEDELL, K., WELTON, J., VORHAUS, G. (1981) *The Assessment of Special Educational Needs*, Report to the DES, copy lodged in the library of the University of London Institute of Education.

WELTON, J. (1982) 'Schools in the welfare network' in *Child Care, Health and Development*, 8, pp. 271–82.

WELTON, J. (1983) 'Pastoral care in the social division of welfare' in *Pastoral Care in Education*, 12, pp. 121–9.

WELTON, J., DWYER, S. (1982) *Schools in the welfare Network*, unpublished report to the Department of Education for Northern Ireland.

WELTON, J., HENDERSON, G. (1980) *Needs, Tasks and Professionalism*, Paper presented to the British Educational Research Association.

WELTON, J., WEDELL, K., VORHAUS, G. (1982) *Meeting Special Educational Needs: the 1981 Education Act and Its Implications*, Bedford Way Paper No. 12, University of London, Institute of Education.

WERTHAMN, C. (1963) 'Delinquents in schools: a test for the legitimacy of authority' in *Berkeley Journal of Sociology*, 8, 1, pp. 39–60

WESTON, P., TAYLOR, P., and HURMAN, A. (1978) 'Clients' expectations of secondary schooling' in *Educational Review*, 30, 2, pp. 159–66.

WESTWOOD, P. (1975) *The Remedial Teachers' Handbook*, Edinburgh, Oliver and Boyd.

WHITE, R. (1980) *Absent Without Cause*, London, Routledge and Kegan Paul.

WILLIAMS, A. (1979) *Basic Subjects for Slow Learners*, London, Methuen.

WILLIAMS, G. (1982) 'The economics of education: current debates and prospects' in *British Journal of Educational Studies*, XXX(1), pp. 97–107.

WILLIS, P. (1980) *Learning to Labour*, Hampshire, Gower.

WILSON, B. (1962) 'The teacher's role — sociological analysis' in *British Journal of Sociology*, 13, pp. 15–31.

WINNICOTT, D. (1958) *Hate in the Counter Transference*, London, Tavistock Publications.

WOODS, P. (1979) *The Divided Schools*, London, Routledge and Kegan Paul.

Notes on Contributors

RON BEST is Principal Lecturer and Head of the Educational Research Centre at Chelmer Institute of Higher Education in Essex. He has published widely on aspects of Pastoral Care in Education, including two books: *Perspectives on Pastoral Care* and *Education and Care* (with Peter Ribbins and others, Heinemann, 1980, 1983). He is a founder member of NAPCE and a member of its executive committee. He is currently researching the organization of remedial provision in the comprehensive school.

KEITH BLACKBURN is the Head of St. George's School, Gravesend. He has made a considerable contribution to the literature of Pastoral Care and associated topics and is the author of two books: *The Tutor* and *Head of House, Head of Year* (Heinemann, 1975, 1983). He is a founder member of NAPCE and was until recently its Deputy Chair and the organizer of its national conferences.

STEVE DECKER is a Senior Lecturer in Educational Psychology at the Chelmer Institute of Higher Education in Essex. He is also co-founder and director of a voluntary counselling agency, the Benfleet Open Door Service. He has worked as a junior school teacher and a local authority Educational Psychologist.

PETER LANG is a Lecturer in Education at the University of Warwick where, for a number of years, he has been running courses in pastoral care at Diploma and M.Ed. levels. He has published many articles on various aspects of pastoral care. He is the co-editor of *New Directions in Pastoral Care in Education* (Blackwells, 1985) and General Editor (with Peter Ribbins) of the forthcoming series *Blackwell's Studies in Pastoral Care and Personal and Social Education*. He is a founder member of NAPCE, currently its Treasurer, and a co-editor of its journal *Pastoral Care in Education*.

ROBERT LASLETT was until recently a Lecturer in the Department of Special Education at the University of Birmingham. He was for several years the Head of a school for maladjusted children. He is the author of three books or monographs: *Educating Maladjusted Children* (1977), *Maladjusted Children in the Ordinary School* (1982) and *Effective Classroom Management* (with Colin Smith, Croom Helm, 1984).

NEVILLE JONES is Principal Educational Psychologist for Oxfordshire. He was editor of the journal *Therapeutic Education* from 1969–79 and has published over thirty articles and chapters on the education and management of children with special needs. He has been a member of the Council and Executive Committee of the NCB, member of the Advisory Committee of NAMH, and is currently member of the Psychological Research Committee of the British Dyslexia Association.

MICHAEL MARLAND is Headmaster of ILEA's North Westminster Community School and Honorary Professor of Education at Warwick University. He combines leading this large multi-campus school with editing *Heinemann Organization in Schools Series* and writing and editing very many books on pastoral care, the curriculum, and aspects of school management. He was the author of *Pastoral Care* (1974), and his most recent books include *Sex Differentiation and Schooling*, *School Management Tasks* and *New Directions in Pastoral Care in Education*. He is the founder Chair of NAPCE; Chairs the Royal Opera House Education Council, and is a member of the ESRCs Education and Human Development Committee.

PETER RIBBINS is a Lecturer in the Department of Social and Administrative Studies in Education at the University of Birmingham. He has published many articles on a wide variety of aspects of the contemporary comprehensive school and is the co-author or co-editor of a number of books and monographs including: *Perspectives on Pastoral Care* and *Education and Care* (with Ron Best and others) and *Managing Education: The System and the Institution* (with Meredydd Hughes and Hywel Thomas, Holt, Rinehart and Winston, 1985). He is general editor (with Peter Lang) of the forthcoming series *Blackwells Studies in Pastoral Care and Personal and Social Education* and is founding executive editor of *Pastoral Care in Education*. He is currently researching into the role of the Subject Department in the Comprehensive School, and into the Careers Service.

HYWEL THOMAS is a Lecturer in the Department of Social and Administrative Studies in Education at the University of Birmingham. He has published a number of papers which seek to apply ideas taken from economics to the study of education management and planning. He is the co-editor of *Research in Educational Management and Administration* and *Managing Education: The System and the Institution*. His most recent research has been into economic aspects of upper secondary provision.

JOHN WELTON is a Lecturer in the Department of Economic, Administrative and Policy Studies in Education of the University of London Institute of Education. He has written widely on various aspects of the organization and management of schooling. He is co-author of *Meeting Special Educational Needs: The 1981 Act and its Implications* (Bedford Way Papers, 1982) and of *Schools in the Welfare Network* (unpublished report of the Department of Education thern Ireland, 1982). He is a member of the Editorial Team and Review Editor for the journal *Education Management and Administration*.

Index